But Children Matter

But Children Matter

Successful Children's Ministry Volunteerism Strategies

Kenneth G. Warren
AND
John S. Knox

FOREWORD BY
Chris Goeppner

AFTERWORD BY
Art and Jenny Matheny

WIPF & STOCK · Eugene, Oregon

BUT CHILDREN MATTER
Successful Children's Ministry Volunteerism Strategies

Copyright © 2020 Kenneth G. Warren and John S. Knox. All rights reserved. Except for brief quotations in critical publications or reviews, no part of this book may be reproduced in any manner without prior written permission from the publisher. Write: Permissions, Wipf and Stock Publishers, 199 W. 8th Ave., Suite 3, Eugene, OR 97401.

Wipf & Stock
An Imprint of Wipf and Stock Publishers
199 W. 8th Ave., Suite 3
Eugene, OR 97401

www.wipfandstock.com

PAPERBACK ISBN: 978-1-5326-8692-4
HARDCOVER ISBN: 978-1-5326-8693-1
EBOOK ISBN: 978-1-5326-8694-8

Scripture quotations are from The ESV® Bible (The Holy Bible, English Standard Version®), copyright © 2001 by Crossway, a publishing ministry of Good News Publishers. Used by permission. All rights reserved.

Manufactured in the U.S.A.   01/13/20

For Ester

Contents

List of Illustrations | viii
Foreword by Chris Goeppner | ix
Preface | xi
Acknowledgements | xiii

1. Introduction to Children's Ministry | 1
2. The Obstacles | 16
3. The Investigation | 31
4. The Discussion | 49
5. The Solution | 77
6. Epilogue | 88

Afterword by Art and Jenny Matheny | 97
Appendices | 101
Bibliography | 117
Index | 121

Illustrations

Figure 1: Ages At Which Americans Accept Christ | 10

Figure 2: Volunteer Survey Responses | 40

Figure 3: Pastoral/Ministry Leader Survey Responses | 40

Figure 4: 12Stone Church Team Process | 72

Figure 5: 12Stone Church Volunteer Handbook | 84

Foreword

Ask any pastor what the most important program is in their church and nearly all would answer the same thing: the children's ministry. In fact, all healthy and growing churches have healthy and growing children's ministries. As church leaders, we ought to be spending time and resources on our children as they are our future leaders.

Wes Stafford, former president of Compassion International, once told me that our programs for kids are the church's greatest leadership pipeline and best discipleship program. If this is true, why do many of our churches struggle in this area and exhibit a lack of excellence? Where can we turn for a fresh view of children's ministry and possible solutions for training and vision?

I have known Kenny Warren for nearly thirty years. He has proven gifting and skills in church leadership and programs. He has studied children's ministry and, more importantly, he has put into practice what he has learned. His extensive research, thorough interviews, and well-drawn conclusions from his doctoral research form the basis of this helpful book.

Kenny (with the assistance of sociologist John S. Knox) lays a firm biblical foundation on the importance of children by examining excerpts from both the Old and New Testaments. From these, he builds to show the blessing of children and the value God places on them.

The history of children's ministry is an outgrowth of this biblical mandate to train and raise children in the "admonition" of the Lord. Sadly, research shows that much of children's ministry over the years has missed the mark, having neither happy servants nor

FOREWORD

the effective transfer of kingdom truths. The cited history indicates that more is needed for this most important ministry area.

Four areas of critical need are highlighted and examined: system, coaching, clarity, and training. Our churches need an effective system to identify and put volunteer servants into place. These servants need coaching and training to be effective and fulfilled in serving children. The church's vision and goals need to be clear so that servants understand the path to a "Win" in children's ministry.

In a volunteer environment, satisfaction of volunteers is directly related to them staying involved in service. The better the training, coaching, and understanding of the vision they have, the better the results will be seen in their area of ministry. The churches spending time in these areas will have happier and better-trained volunteers, which impact children in many positive ways.

As a pastor and a close friend of the author, I highly recommend you check out this book. If you want to understand and improve your church's teaching and training of children, Kenny's research and insight will help and assist. With so much at stake, we must strive to introduce our kids to Jesus early in life, to equip them to serve Christ faithfully, to assist families in creating more Godly homes, and to raise up future leaders in our churches. May God bless Kenny and John's book in these endeavors!

Chris Goeppner
Lead and Founding Pastor
Riverbank Church

Preface

I have flown many times and it has always been an effective and quick (at least once in the air) means of travel. Flying is something that I have never been crazy about, but, for the most part, there has always been a feeling of safety in the air—minus a few situations where there was some turbulence and one unnerving incident (while over the Atlantic Ocean) caused by a gentleman who was vaping in the restroom. Smoke alarms going off in the middle of the night on a plane that was at full capacity with passengers was nerve racking, to say the least.

Despite this, I felt safe because the airplane—whether a 777 or a 727—was built to be in the skies for long periods of time. I felt safe because the airline staff had all been properly trained. I felt safe because—whether a three hundred or four hundred person flight—all the passengers on the plane mattered to the airline company.

Unlike some of the air travel experiences that I have encountered, many of my observations surrounding children's ministry experiences that I have been a part of were not like my airplane voyages. Often, these experiences were more like being on a plane that was not quite ready to fly. I cannot imagine taking off in a plane with only one engine, a cracked windshield or, worse yet, a flight crew that had been ill-trained to facilitate a safe flight for passengers. It may be possible for this to happen, but who would want to be on this flight? The chances of a safety issue arising would seem too high, indeed. Everyone aboard would prefer a smooth flight and a gentle landing to a fearful, agitated journey ending only with a crash landing, damaged plane, and hurt passengers.

PREFACE

Similarly, in far too many cases, it seems as though churches prepare for ministry in ways that will not ensure that they soar as a ministry. It is as if some ministries are of greater importance than others. It is as if they think that some ministries can be developed or improved when the plane is in the air rather than safely on the ground. It is as if ministry leaders sometimes communicate that children matter (but only behind the scenes); however,

1. not as much as the median adults in the church because, after all, only the adults contribute, financially.
2. not as much as the senior adults because of their socially prominent position and role in the church community infrastructure.
3. not as much as the music ministry because, after all, the church has to provide a quality worship experience.
4. not as much as the building program because, after all, the church needs to provide state of the art facilities.

This book encourages church leaders to take children's ministry to another level because the truth is that children are a crucial matter to the kingdom. They matter to God, and the future of the church hinges upon their development. In a short time, these children will become the adults who will be the *engine* of the church. As such, they deserve the best in terms of volunteer development and an overall quality ministry experience that others in the church are experiencing.

My hope is that the concepts and ideas in this book will motivate church leaders to take a long, hard look at the children's ministry in their church. Is your ministry ready for take-off or is your church stuck and simply in "maintenance mode" when it comes to children's ministry?

Kenny Warren
Doctor of Ministry
Liberty University

Acknowledgements

First, to my great wife, Ester, I thank you for your loving support as I completed this project. I am blessed to have a great wife like you. It was your service in children's ministry that was the catalyst that influenced me to write on this topic. In addition to being an awesome wife (and mother), you are also the best children's ministry volunteer that I have ever known.

Second, to my children, Bailey and Molly: I am blessed to be your father. Thank you for allowing me the long nights of writing and the encouraging words that you provided to support my efforts with this project. I am so excited for your future and all that God has in store for you.

Next, to all the children's ministry volunteers in the U.S. and across the globe: thank you for your ministry to children and for your part in building the kingdom of God. I pray that every church will see the tremendous value that you bring to Christian ministry and that efforts will be made to equip you for even greater ministry in the days ahead.

Also, I send special thanks to Dan Burrell. Thank you so much for your guidance and feedback with this project. I believe that God used you to provide precise words of encouragement and support, which kept me going and made all the difference in my completing this project. I greatly appreciate all that you did for me in your role as my mentor.

ACKNOWLEDGEMENTS

Finally, I want to offer special thanks to Justin Silvey. Your influence in my life proved to be critical in my completing this project. God truly used our friendship and this project was an example of iron sharpening iron. Your scholarly critique and erudite consultation made this project better.

Sincerely,
Kenny

1

Introduction

In far too many churches and ministries in America, children's ministry volunteers are relegated to the end of the line in terms of training, development, and care provided by church staff members or church leaders. Danny Watterson states, "There's also a gap in leadership development of children's ministry volunteers. For too long, the mentality has been to find people who will babysit the kids on Sunday mornings."[1]

Although many pastors and church leaders excel in terms of finding and developing volunteers for their children's ministries, they still struggle with the important aspects of the ministry, including training, recruiting and retention. It is not uncommon to hear an announcement and/or desperate plea from the Sunday morning church pulpit for children's ministry volunteers. As Jesus said in Matthew 9:35-38, "The harvest is plentiful, but the laborers are few." Sadly, the cries for Christian volunteers are seldom fruitful and leave ministry leaders chronically frustrated and puzzled over solutions for finding shepherds for the littlest in the flock.

Scripture is very clear that children matter to God, as evidenced by passages such as Psalm 127:3-5, where God says, "Behold, children are a heritage from the LORD, the fruit of the womb a reward. Like arrows in the hand of a warrior are the children of one's youth. Blessed is the man who fills his quiver with them! He shall not be put to shame when he speaks with his enemies in the gate."[2]

---

1. Watterson, "Why High Capacity Children's Pastors."
2. Unless otherwise noted, all biblical passages referenced are in the English Standard Version (ESV).

Additionally, the Gospels provide a clear example of Jesus becoming angered because of the way his own Disciples were treating children whom were hoping to interact with Him. In Mark 10:13–16, Jesus states,

> And they were bringing children to Him that He might touch them, and the disciples rebuked them. But when Jesus saw it, He was indignant and said to them, "Let the children come to me; do not hinder them, for to such belongs the kingdom of God. Truly, I say to you, whoever does not receive the kingdom of God like a child shall not enter it." And He took them in His arms and blessed them, laying His hands on them.

Although the heart of a child might be unimportant (or repugnant) to some in Christian social circles, for God, the realm of Heaven is a perfect fit for these children's hearts of trust, hope, and celebration.

The Old Testament and Children

By studying Old Testament history, one can easily see the fundamental value that was placed on children, manifested in Exodus, Leviticus, and Deuteronomy. There is little direct prescription in these books on parenting tactics, but much indirect evidence is presented suggesting that children are to be included and active participant in a loving, caring, faith community.[3] The church has a pivotal role in the development of children, which is so much more than a Sunday school lesson each week. Children's ministry volunteers assist in children's cognitive, social, and, of course, spiritual growth. Although faith communities today may look quite dissimilar compared to those of the Old Testament, the quintessential role of the church community in ministering to children (as implied in the Old Testament) has certainly not changed.

According to May,

---

3. Richards, *Children's Ministry*, 18.

INTRODUCTION

Moses' instructions in Deuteronomy were given to the whole faith community. Parents and children were to talk about and live out God's commands and keep their feasts in the home. But they would also gather for corporate celebrations of the feasts and observe other families in the community living God's laws.[4]

One wonders how much of the downward spiral of morality in society today can be attributed to the lack of ministry to children in the church, which is, of course, almost exclusively done by volunteers. Is the church engaged in truly aiding children's cognitive development? Are leaders and teachers helping children think about the decisions they are making and decisions they will need to make in the future?

For example, Old Testament history does not provide readers with the exact role of the faith community in the life of the Prophet Daniel. Although he is most famous for his experience in the lion's den (Daniel 6), his cognitive and ethical prowess was the product of a solid parental foundation, and also one honed in a strong faith community. When he was taken into Babylonian captivity and offered the king's food and wine (something forbidden by Jewish culture), Daniel refused.

The scriptures record Daniel's response to the King's offer in Daniel 1:8: "But Daniel resolved not to defile himself with the royal food and wine, and he asked the chief official for permission not to defile himself this way." The resolve that this prophet displayed did not just magically spring up on its own; it was something that had been cultivated in Daniel, beginning with a personal relationship with God, and developed in him through the faith community.

At some point in his rearing, Daniel had been trained to think about being in a situation such as the one that he found himself in, and he was able to be decisive and righteous despite his circumstances. Daniel knew where the boundaries were, and he had evidently decided in advance that he was not going to displease God—even if it meant the loss of his life. In that crisis moment, the scriptures do not depict an individual fractured by indecision and

---

4. May, *Children Matter*, 165–66.

doubt; Daniel's brave choices reflect a strong character and integrity that was grounded and fortified in faith and fellowship.

This resolve from Daniel can be observed in the account of the lion's den in Daniel 6:1–28. An interesting component of Daniel's development is the social aspect of the commitment that Daniel displayed along with his friends Shadrach, Meshach, and Abed-Nego. Although these men appear to have benefited from a strong foundation like Daniel, readers can also perceive the contagious nature of Daniel's righteousness and courage being displayed in chapter one.

Daniel's influence on his friends represents another important impact of children's ministry and the volunteers ministering within those programs. When children are developed well, they bond well with others who have a similar resolve or are willing to be used by God as catalysts to increase the level of resolve and commitment to Christ in others (just as Daniel's three friends would later do in their exhilarating journey).

With Daniel, it is obvious that his spiritual development also affected the cognitive and social aspects of his life, which is something every children's ministry volunteer needs to comprehend. The impact being made in the cognitive, social, and spiritual realms within a child is significant.

Jesus and Children

When exploring this matter in the New Testament era, one can see that Jesus felt strongly about how people treated children. As mentioned earlier, Mark 10:13–16 reveals that Jesus became angry when some Disciples viewed and treated children as being insignificant. According to Keeley, "This is one of only two incidents in which Jesus is shown to become angry."[5] The anger demonstrated by Jesus shows that Jesus was passionate about children and their spiritual development.

---

5. Keeley, *Helping Our Children*, 45.

INTRODUCTION

Jesus knew the importance of children coming to a saving faith at a young age. By example, Jesus demonstrated to the Disciples (and all future generations) that ministry to children should be a high priority and that children should have no obstacles preventing them from approaching God. Even today, if an individual does not embrace the Christian faith in childhood, the likelihood that they will receive Christ is significantly reduced through their remaining years.

A History of Children's Ministry Volunteerism

Medieval Era

Much of the early church ministry to children—apart from what is portrayed in the writings in the Gospels—is minimal. The primary responsibility for spiritual development of children was laid at the feet of their parents. Some of the first individuals outside of parents or, one might say, the first children's ministry volunteers, came onto the scene during the Medieval Era of the church (500–1350 CE). These years (and those leading into the Middle Ages) were lacking in the development of lay ministry to children beyond the parental responsibility to train children in the care and admonition of the Lord. Visual learning was the most frequently used tactic for developing the faith of children.[6]

The Medieval Era provides a snapshot of some of the earliest children's ministry volunteers recorded:

> The times were dangerous for children, with many dying in infancy. Christian parents feared—and their fears were amplified by the church—that if their child died without being baptized, the child would be eternally condemned. Since clergy were not always present when a baby was deathly ill, laypeople were given instruction so that in an emergency they could perform a baptism.[7]

---

6. May, *Children Matter*, 94.
7. May, *Children Matter*, 95.

Although this may not have been the ideal way for a children's ministry volunteer to minister, it appears to be one of the first recorded instances of a lay worker engaging in a form of ministry to children.

Renaissance and Reformation

Next in the history of children's ministry were the ages of the Renaissance and Reformation (1350–1650 CE). During these centuries, the way that children were nurtured began to shift away from parenting alone to one more of a community approach. The influence of parents was not minimized, but the role that the community played in the children's development was intensified and expanded. The great reformer Martin Luther was a central figure in this era of church history, and he noted that the elasticity of the child and preadolescent functions as ideal soil in which to plant important ideas of faith.

More so than any other time in life, these formative years of childhood are critical in establishing the foundation for a faithful adulthood.[8] A recognition of the importance of nurturing children began to emerge during this era, and, as mentioned earlier, some cultural shifting occurred in terms of the roles and influences of key members of society concerning the spiritual development of children.

The Early Modern Period

An additional shift in the development of children came during the Early Modern Period (1700–1900 CE). This era was marked by a transition that was inspired by the Industrial Revolution. This revolution led to an increased number of families leaving rural communities for the larger cities of America. A growing number of parents entered the workforce, which brought new challenges and educational obstacles to many children. Schools

---

8. May, *Children Matter*, 97.

started to assist with the rising needs of children—many of whom were living on the streets or not receiving the care that they should have been because their parents were absent, exhausted, or even the children themselves had entered the workforce. This period also marked the beginning of the Sunday school ministry of the church, which was in large part started to reach the children described above.[9]

Although started by Robert Raikes, the outreach arm of Sunday school spread through the leadership of a Baptist draper named William Fox. Fox developed what would be called the Sunday School Society in order to promote the concept of the Sunday school.[10] It is worth noting that although the Sunday school is generally considered a volunteer effort, the Sunday School Society teachers recruited by the society were paid through funds collected by Fox.[11]

Before the nineteenth century, John Wesley, the founder of the Methodist movement (and eventually the church), continued to propel the Sunday school movement.[12] Wesley saw great value and opportunity to reach and teach children for the advancement of the kingdom of God. According to Knox, "Wesley started to utilize the laity in his ministry, adding to the disdain of the Anglican Church, which criticized the dangerous lack of education of many of Wesley's appointed lay preachers."[13] Still, Wesley understood the potential of volunteerism as did others, leading to the creation of groups such the American Sunday School Union in 1824.

The Modern Period

By the 1900s, the Sunday school movement grew to the point that "at least 32 million Americans regularly participate[d] in a

---

9. May, *Children Matter*, 97.
10. Power, *Rise and Progress*, 73.
11. May, *Children Matter*, 102.
12. May, *Children Matter*, 102.
13. Knox, *John Wesley's 52 Standard Sermons*, 16.

Sunday school program."[14] At this time, there were essentially no paid Sunday school workers as there were in the day of Robert Raikes. The Sunday school became a powerful force in the twentieth century and was mentioned as being the largest volunteer force in the entire world, with people serving long hours and continuing to serve to influence children and their families with the gospel of Jesus Christ.[15] One of the great differences in modern children's ministries (versus those of the past) is the wide array of ministry that is now offered to children, requiring an increasing number and variety of children's ministry volunteers needed to assist these programs.

Today, there has been a resurgence of house churches, small group ministries, and a greater movement toward ministries that do not include a Sunday school model. There are still some prominent children's clubs such as A.W.A.N.A.[16] and Word of Life. Within these programs, volunteers can minister effectively to children although the influence of (and attendance in) are waning due in part to the decreased number of services in churches and the rise of the simple church model, which reduces the number of worship opportunities.

One negative effect of the shift of churches to a simpler model of ministry is the fewer number of opportunities available for children's ministry and the volunteers who seek to minister to children. Although Sunday school ministries still have their place and are certainly developing children spiritually, these new ministries are beginning to make their mark in church life. It remains to be seen how the changes in church worship and programming will positively or negatively impact children's ministries.

Some experts view the current movement of the church negatively in terms of church programming. Ivy Beckwith states, "I believe many churches have lost a sense of what the corporate worship of God is all about. It is no longer the centerpiece of

---

14. May, *Children Matter*, 109.
15. May, *Children Matter*, 109.
16. This is an abbreviation of "Approved Workmen Are Not Ashamed."

INTRODUCTION

community life, and this is reflected in how a church views the necessity of a child's participation in it."[17]

Like Beckwith, others seem to be concerned that the emphasis on entertainment or performance that is sweeping through many churches has and will continue to reduce the opportunities for children to be developed through the ministries of the church. This risk is especially true if the churches' overwhelming focus is consistently focused on the worship service alone and not on developing other ministries within the church. Beckwith argues that this model challenges the place of children in terms of what worship ought to be and the inclusion of children in it.[18]

Regardless of the mode of worship that a church uses, there will still be a need for volunteers to help develop children. This need will be different than in the past because facilities are different, with groups meeting in homes and sometimes small rented buildings. Moreover, as noted earlier, the amount of time people spend at church is decreasing due to the limited numbers of opportunities that churches are offering throughout the week. This could be the beginning of history repeating itself and the complete role of the spiritual development of children returning to parents. For now, children's ministry volunteers continue to play a vital role in the spiritual and social development of children through the local church.

Importance of Ministry to Children

In his investigations and reporting, George Barna "stresses the importance of children's ministry by contending that lifelong moral views are largely in place by adolescence. 'What you believe at age thirteen is pretty much what you're going to die believing.'"[19] Research compiled by the Barna Group shows that children between the ages of five and thirteen have a 32 percent

---

17. Beckwith, *Postmodern Children's Ministry*, 143.
18. Beckwith, *Postmodern Children's Ministry*, 143.
19. Kennedy, "4–14 Window."

9

probability of accepting Jesus Christ as their Savior. That likelihood drops to 4 percent for teenagers between the ages of fourteen and eighteen, and ticks back up to 6 percent for adults older than eighteen. Table 1 reveals how critical it is for children to be reached with the gospel.[20]

TABLE 1

Age	Conversions (%)
0–3	1
4–14	85
15–30	10
30+	4

Figure 1: Ages At Which Americans Accept Christ

Although Proverbs 22:6 speaks to the parents' role of training children, the church also has a responsibility to come alongside parents to aid them in the spiritual development of their children. If children are truly being trained up in the way they should go, then there should be more fruit of training than what is often observed. According to David Kinnaman, reporting on a 2011 Barna nationwide survey, he notes that some "59 percent of young people with a Christian background report that they had or have 'dropped out of attending church, after going regularly.'"[21]

No one has forced these youths to leave the church, but with statistics this elevated, there must be numerous reasons that these students did not remain plugged into a local body. It is also possible that many of the 59 percent who left the church did not have a personal relationship with Christ to begin with—thus increasing the number of those who navigated their way through church ministries only to eventually leave the church altogether. The question remains on whether this reveals something about

---

20. Kennedy, "4–14 Window."
21. Kinnaman and Hawkins, *You Lost Me*, 23.

INTRODUCTION

the quality (or lack of quality) of children's ministry volunteerism that churches are developing.

For many of these students, it is likely that there may not have been a strong relational connection to either a children's ministry pastor or volunteer during this time. If there was such a bond, it may have been with a low-impact children's ministry volunteer (meaning a volunteer who lacked the calling, training, or even passion to fulfill this important ministry role). Regardless, one could deduce that children may not be getting ministered to in a way that resonants with them enough to cause them to want to remain connected to the local church.

Since the responsibility to spiritually prepare children lies in part with the church as previously asserted, this survey is revealing, as some of the one thousand participants were likely nonbelievers. Once again, parents bear the primary responsibility for the spiritual development of their children, but when considering Proverbs 22:6—"Train up a child in the way he should go; even when he is old he will not depart from it"—one can surmise that even the most learned parent does not have all the answers for the spiritual development of their children.

The church, if allowed by parents, can come alongside and provide great support in this important effort. Testimonies are available that speak to the success of children's ministry volunteers in their partnership, with parents in raising spiritually strong children. However, these participants are seemingly noticing a decline in the morality of children while not necessarily seeing the role the church plays in the moral development in the lives of children.

Thus,

> Children's church support is also likely to impact their spiritual formation because one's connection to God is developed and maintained through reciprocal spiritual support within the church community, and one's perception of God is influenced by those relationships. In fact, prior research has found significant correlations between adults' spirituality and the quality of their relationships with other people in the church. Limited research with adolescents has also shown a link between positive

spiritual development with intimate, intentional relationships with a church youth pastor.[22]

The implication here is that most children's ministry volunteers have not been equipped sufficiently to personally connect with children in such a way that the children cultivate a love for Christ and his church. The sad ultimate effect of this absence of equipping is that many of these same children will one day say goodbye to the church for an extended period of time, if not forever.

As Crosby and Smith remark,

> The majority of churches have only a vague notion of what they are trying to accomplish with their children and families. At worst, some congregations have "time slots" that they fill with a variety of activities that are appealing to children and parents. However, the programs often are not connected with each other in any way even though they are ministering to the same group of children. Teachers seldom are aware of the content of other ministries, and sometimes they are rotating in and out of classes, even unaware of what was taught or experienced in the previous session of the same ministry.[23]

In a national survey of over one thousand children and teens, of whom over six hundred had been involved in Sunday school on a consistent basis, Ken Ham discovered that "the church had failed these people miserably. As children and teenagers, these children were present every Sunday; they were committed and they were present; they heard the lesson and they nodded their heads ... and it had a nominal and even negative effect on their faith."[24] This suggests that the church, in many cases, may not be fully prepared to execute one of the most important aspects of church ministry, that being children's ministry.

If this is the case (in any given church), it is not God's ideal. It is not a picture of excellence, which is what the church should be demonstrating toward its most valuable commodity. It has the

---

22. Crosby and Smith, "Church Support as a Predictor," 243–54.
23. Haywood, *Enduring Connections*, 7.
24. Ham et al., *Already Gone*, 44.

INTRODUCTION

potential to harm the cause of Christ; and, finally, it is a violation of Ephesians 4:11–12 where Paul instructs church leaders to "equip the saints for the work of ministry."

As Wuest notes, "These gifted men are given the church 'for the perfecting of the saints.' The word 'perfecting' is *katartizō* (καταρτίζω), 'to equip for service.' These gifted men are to specialize in equipping the saints for 'the work of the ministry', that is, for ministering work, in short, Christian service."[25] Unfortunately, this lack of equipping is typically not viewed as a travesty and continues in some churches because making this ministry work requires time, effort, and resources that church leaders sometimes believe would be better implemented in other parts of the ministry.

The ultimate purpose of a local church ministry is to point everyone, but especially children, toward Christ for salvation while also carrying out the beginning steps of discipleship as they learn what it means to be a follower of Christ. Unfortunately, as George Barna points out,

> It develops its own persona and ministry niche within the community, the ministry to children generally takes a backseat to the more visible and adult-oriented efforts of the church. Within a decade of holding its first public service, the average church relegates children's ministry to holding-tank status, seeking to keep parents happy, kids occupied, denominational executives and the church's reputation (i.e., that it offers adequate service in all of the fundamental areas of ministry) intact.[26]

Churches often have great intentions and joy in communicating how much children are a priority. Yet, as time passes and the demands of ministry increase, the perceived importance of developing a children's ministry that is life-changing for the children involved and the volunteers who serve in this area often wanes. There is a state of contentment that surfaces in which leadership believes this ministry is adequate, but in all reality, the underlying primary focus remains on the adult ministries of the church.

---

25. Wuest, *Wuest's Word Studies*, 101.
26. Barna, *Transforming Children*, 96.

As the focus on children's ministry diminishes, the development of volunteers drifts, qualifications for serving are reduced, the vision for this ministry is communicated less, and leadership satisfaction increases for the children's ministry becoming a "holding tank" with children's ministry volunteers babysitting more than the ministering. As this pattern continues, children's ministry volunteers become disillusioned with their church work. They comprehend the fact that God loves children and that Jesus loves children, but they are no longer convinced that their own church loves children the way that the institutional church (and Bible) might have once communicated.

With this said, in recent years, there has been a dramatic increase in church plants and house churches, which now dot the landscape of North America. Traditional church buildings have been substituted with houses or with schools or other more affordable options due to churches thinking more strategically and practically to best meet the needs of the church. Non-traditional buildings could lead some churches to forgo a strong effort to build children's ministry programming because of spacing issues or other dynamics associated with starting a new church.

This could complicate or impede the development of children's ministry programming and alter the role of children's ministry volunteers. This book primarily reveals the issues, struggles, and problems associated with established churches, or those two years old and older. However, the plans described later to improve the impact of children's ministry workers will apply to any church.

Often, a disconnect exists between how pastors, children's ministry volunteers, and churches describe the health and impact of children's ministry volunteers and the overall functioning of an ongoing children's ministry. The volunteer dysfunction that is evident in many churches goes beyond the building scenario or the current strategy that leadership is pursuing. If one asks the pastor of just about any local church how the children's ministry is going, most pastors will respond positively. They will typically make remarks such as "Our folks do a great job with our kids," or "Great things are happening in the lives of our children." However,

INTRODUCTION

if speaking with a children's ministry volunteer, one is likely to hear, "I am burned out, but I feel obligated to serve here because we have such a shortage of volunteers and I do love these kids."

The sentiments above are dangerous in several ways. A pastor should be positive about all ministries, including children's ministry, but like other ministries, difficult questions need to be asked frequently to determine the health of the ministry and the ministry volunteer. On the lay side, it is difficult to see how a children's ministry volunteer or any other volunteer could impact the kingdom with the state of ministry that the fictional volunteer comment above describes. So often, there is no system in place to monitor the health of the ministry. There is no accountability other than "are they present." Official training is lacking, church vision is blurred, and many children's ministry volunteers feel like they are nothing more than large-group, unpaid babysitters.

Attempting to describe the reasons churches fail to develop children's ministry volunteers is somewhat daunting because the church is as diverse today as it has ever been. Also, while many churches are failing in the area of developing children's ministry volunteers, there are many who are raising up healthy and high-impact volunteers who are making a difference in their local church. According to Heather Ingersoll, "While adult's desires are important, the church will never reach a more balanced approach to nurturing children's spirituality without placing a greater emphasis on the perspective of the needs of children."[27] In other words, children matter and there are options among the obstacles.

27. Ingersoll, "Making Room."

2

The Obstacles

This book outlines steps that churches can take to develop local children's ministry volunteerism so that the church is built up, the volunteer is equipped, and children are spiritually impacted as a result of the volunteer's service. Furthermore, we sought to examine and compare data from senior ministry leaders (as well as children's ministry volunteers) to identify areas of health and weakness in this area of ministry. It is imperative that churches continue to develop children's ministry volunteers for several important reasons. Children need to know that the church values them by empowering and equipping leaders who will assist children in becoming all that God desires for them.

It is also important that volunteers who have been called by God to serve in children's ministry receive ongoing support from their local church and have a vision provided by church leadership. Children's ministry volunteers and the children served by these volunteers at a minimum deserve this much. Our study communicates the church's need to develop children's ministry volunteers and exposes current weaknesses in this area of ministry while providing principles that will develop this ministry and ultimately bring honor and glory to Christ.

The Project's Scope and Limitations

It is easy to see the difficulties facing many churches in the area of children's ministry, and although a plan to develop high impact children's ministry volunteers is introduced in this book, it

THE OBSTACLES

is impossible to develop a plan that fits every local church due to the unique needs presented in churches across the country. This study is limited in that much of the research stems from survey data responses of pastors and church leaders located exclusively along the East Coast of the United States. Additionally, some of the church leadership surveys were completed by laity rather than clergy since many children's ministry leaders are unpaid—thus, possibly offering a different perspective than responses from paid church staff. The surveys were completed in late 2013 and early 2014, with the first draft of this manuscript being completed in early 2018. This elapsed time could have in some way changed the answers provided by participants but is not likely.

As we sought pastoral participants, many were hesitant to have their volunteers participate in the survey as they seemed somewhat threatened by the questions outlined in this work. This resulted in a lower number of completed surveys than what we had hoped. Yet, as with other investigative studies of religiosity and praxis, "The surveys might have been considered too long, the project not a high priority, or perhaps considered an invasion of privacy."[1]

This book is not a training or "how-to" guide for churches. Nor is it a step-by-step handbook for churches to put into place. The information found in these chapters will primarily be of value to churches trying to strengthen children's ministry volunteers.

Methodological Approach

We hope to encourage the development of children's ministry volunteers in the local church through a study of modern experts and scholars who have shown dedication to improving the children's ministry volunteer experience or the general volunteer experience for both individuals and churches. One of this study's goals was to compare the views of pastors and volunteers about the children's

1. Knox, *Sacro-Egoism*, 35.

ministry in which they serve to determine whether this ministry of the church is functioning in a healthy manner. This was done through surveys that were sent to numerous children's ministry volunteers along the East Coast of the United States as well as to pastors and children's ministry leaders.

The purpose of these surveys was to discover points of health (as well as dysfunction) within children's ministries in these churches. A second goal was to examine what churches across the country are doing to experience success in their children's ministries in terms of healthy volunteer experiences with growing children's ministries. Some churches are rising above others in this area, and this section of the project sought to uncover some principles that contribute to healthy, high-impact children's ministry volunteers who make a difference for the kingdom. The final goal of this book is to reveal principles and methods that can be used by any church that desires to develop children's ministry volunteers.

Review of Literature

There has been a great deal written about children's ministry volunteers with almost every writer focusing at least somewhat on the importance of children's ministry volunteers (or workers as they are sometimes referred to in their writings). For many years, churches sought to primarily minister to children through paid staff, but due to declining church attendance and the 2008 economic downturn, many churches are revisiting the notion that ministry volunteers are crucial to the success of ministry in general, but especially children's ministry. Sadly, this perspective shift seems to have been birthed out of the loss of finances rather than the concept that less staff and increased laity in this area is espoused by Scripture as the model for churches. Much of the following literature will reveal the benefits that a high-impact volunteer brings to a child who is being ministered to as well as the body of Christ as a whole.

One notable article was written by ministry volunteer expert Al Newell of Newell and Associates. In "Seven Reasons Why Volunteer Ministries Fail," Newell unpacks the most common mistakes that ministry leaders make that often end up destroying the health of the volunteer ministry that they actually trying to help. Al Newell is a leading expert on volunteering in the world and is a former adjunct professor at Denver Seminary, where he taught classes on church volunteerism. He now serves on a fulltime basis by offering seminars for churches and organizations across the country that desire the best from their volunteers and are concerned about retention from an organizational standpoint.

Newell and Associates partners with some of the largest nonprofit organizations in the country such as Samaritan's Purse as well as some of the largest churches in the country and assists them strategically and biblically in developing volunteers for ministries and organizations. We were blessed to be able to attend one of the seminars in 2007, and he was very influential on the topic, exposing many of the fallacies that had previously been perceived as normal. Interestingly, many of the mistakes in volunteer ministries are not carried out by the volunteers, but often are the result of a poor view of senior volunteer leaders in both churches and other nonprofit organizations.

The next work to be discussed focuses specifically on the ministry of children is George Barna's *Transforming Children into Spiritual Champions*. This work is geared toward encouraging the church to come alongside parents for the purpose of assisting them with developing a biblical worldview. Barna's main point is that the church plays a role in cultivating children who will later become spiritual champions for Christ. Therefore, Barna instructs churches to move some of the ministry focus off of adults and onto the children.

In other words, he believes children should be more of a primary ministry focus of the church rather than the lower priority that they often are for many people. Barna explains why children matter and why the church needs to seize opportunities in this area of ministry now rather than waiting. His book is research-based and describes how children can be reached through the church more effectively.

Tony Morgan and Tim Stevens focus on the development of volunteers in their book, *Simply Strategic Volunteers*. This book serves as a practical guide for developing volunteers in a local church. They offer over ninety suggestions for ways churches can elevate their volunteer ministries. Many of the suggestions in the book are commonsense, but are often avoided or not practiced in the local church. Although the book is not directed specifically at children's ministry volunteers, the principles for volunteer development apply to this area of ministry.

A work that has also added great value to this project is Keely's book, *Helping Our Children Grow in Faith*. In this work, Keeley emphasizes the need for the church to take seriously the concept of partnering with parents in order to spiritually nurture children. He returns to the roots of the Jewish culture in which Jesus grew up in order to discover how and why many in the community helped with the raising of children. Keeley provides many illustrations about how this can be accomplished. On another note, he also sheds light on how Jesus valued children and how the church of Jesus Christ should model the example that He provided.

In Jim Wideman's book, *Children's Ministry Volunteers That Stick*, he provides an action plan for churches to develop children's ministry volunteers who thrive in their roles. Wideman offers practical steps for churches to ensure that this happens rather than people just hoping that it happens in the local church.

One of the most impactful parts of the book is where Wideman explores some fifteen different ways in which Jesus developed volunteers. A portion of the book focuses on how having individuals in place who are gifted for specific areas of ministry is the key to fulfillment for the volunteer and ensures productivity from the volunteer within his or her realm of service.

In an effort to continue to expound upon the role of the church in developing children spiritually, Lawrence Richards's *A Theology of Children's Ministry* provides readers with insights into the cognitive development of children. The book is research-based and uncovers the impact of adults on the learning potential of children and shows readers how the church can have a great impact on children through effective education. This work further bolsters the need for trained and committed children's ministry volunteers in the local church to carry out the work being discussed in this project. Richards further describes the goals of an effective children's ministry should be, and how they should be implemented by church leaders and volunteers.

Since there is a strong likelihood that a child's positive or negative children's ministry experience is based on his or her interaction with a children's ministry volunteers or paid staff, the need for leaders to be in place who are actively seeking to glorify God, obey His calling, and use their gifts is paramount. Scott Thomas and Tom Wood reveal the need for leadership coaching in their book, *Gospel Coach: Shepherding Leaders to Glorify God*. Every ministry volunteer needs a coach, and many churches are embracing this concept, realizing that with proper coaching volunteers can go further faster and accomplish more for the kingdom of God as a result.

In the book, the authors explain why every leader needs a coach, but more importantly, why every leader needs what the authors call a "Gospel coach," which is the most effective way to grow and develop volunteers and ministry leaders. Although the concept of coaching children's ministry volunteers is almost unheard of in most churches, the thoughts shared in this book add value to this project because they can bring increased quality and excellence to the ministry of children and highly impact children's ministry volunteers.

David Kinnaman's book, *You Lost Me: Why Young Christians Are Leaving the Church*, is also an important work, as consideration is given to poor training and overall poor efforts from churches to provide quality ministry to children. In this work, Kinnaman highlights areas in which young adults are skeptical of Christianity and all that goes along with being a Christ-follower. These include doubts about the authority of Scripture and individuals who have influenced Christianity through the years. There is a call from Kinnaman in the book for church leaders to embrace the challenges that this skepticism contributes in the form of young adults leaving the church.

In *Building Children's Ministry: A Practical Guide,* Tina Houser describes in detail how a children's ministry should be developed. Special emphasis is placed on volunteer recruitment, retention, and training that needs to take place for ongoing volunteer development. Houser highlights some of the key areas where churches lack proficiency as they prepare and execute a weekly children's ministry. The book challenges churches to place an emphasis on providing excellent children's ministries while pointing out that excellence cannot be bypassed by church leadership. A portion of the book is dedicated to differing volunteer profiles, some of which can be challenging for leaders to empower.

Postmodern Children's Ministry: Ministry to Children in the 21st Century, by Ivy Beckwith, is a work that challenges church leaders in their education ministry to children. Beckwith believes the church has lost its way in some regard with how children are educated in the church. Beckwith describes the importance of children connecting through community within the local church. The ability to connect to the church at a young age is vitally important both during childhood but also as the child matures into adulthood. Beckwith implies in the book that there is too much entertainment and not enough ministry in today's children's programs, which hinders the spiritual development of children and their connection to the church.

With the knowledge and experience gained over thirty years of children's ministry (and in various publishing roles around the country), Beckwith sees children's ministry as something that is broken in many churches. Written by someone who has a passion for and knows the pulse of children's ministry, this book offers solutions for churches and ministry leaders.

Janice Haywood's *Enduring Connections: A Children's Ministry that Weaves* is another work that exposes some of the issues in children's ministry today. In her book, Haywood challenges the church about the value that is placed on children. If churches do indeed value children, she believes that proper equipping and training of volunteers will be highly important to senior church leaders and those directly overseeing children's ministry. Additionally, Haywood asks several important questions to challenge churches to look at the processes in place to see if there are clear steps for children to take as they move forward in their spiritual development and overall walk with Christ.

Examining crucial aspects of volunteer management and engagement in his article, "Moderating Effects of Identification on Volunteer Engagement," Minjeong Kang provides data about the importance of volunteers in society. Although the article is not directly tied to church ministry, the value of volunteers shines through in this article as Kang sheds light on the economic and manpower implications of volunteers in the nonprofit sector. One of Kang's primary points is that because volunteers are so incredibly valuable, there are keys as to how organizations should treat them, with insights gathered as to how the volunteer themselves wish to be treated by the organization.

Through his surveys, Kang gathered data from almost two thousand volunteers who were working with prison ministries in the northeastern part of the United States. Kang discovered that the greater the identity or the connection was between the organization and the volunteer, the greater the level of satisfaction, commitment, affect, engagement, and feeling of empowerment as the volunteers committed their time and resources to this cause.

Stanley, Joiner, and Jones's book, *7 Practices of Effective Ministry*, is a classic in terms of how the church should be organized for ministry. It contributes greatly to the need for appropriate communication in the church setting, which is something that can create volunteer apathy if not handled correctly or volunteer momentum if handled well. Studying Andy Stanley's North Point Community Church, it is obvious that volunteers love serving at this church. The church has created a pipeline of volunteers through communicating vision along with clear steps for volunteers to begin serving.

At North Point, no one will hear a church leader begging for volunteers because there is a strong connection between the church vision and service opportunities at the church. Individuals at North Point know when they are "winning" because it has been clarified for them; they never have to guess if they are making an impact for the cause of Christ. Nothing is more frustrating for volunteers in any part of a ministry or organization than for the goals and values of the church or organization to lack clarity. In time, this proves to be detrimental to the volunteer's development and often leads to the volunteer eventually moving away from service, at least in the area of service where there is a lack of clarity.

In his book, Stanley refers to the process of communicating goals and values as "clarifying the win" for churches that are dependent on individuals serving as volunteers. Stanley implies that this clarification assists the church or organization with motivating volunteers and keeping everyone moving forward in unison. It is rather amazing but also sad that in many congregations, those who serve have an unclear idea of why they are doing what they are doing. Rarely will one receive the same answer if ten different volunteers were asked the same question.

In many cases, volunteers are unable to connect the vision of the church with the service they are giving to the Lord through His church. This one principle (if followed or implemented) has the potential to reenergize children's ministry volunteers throughout the country as well as to improve the retention rate of children's ministry volunteers.

The final two sources provide strategies for the development of children's ministry volunteers, including incorporating both coaching and teamwork into ministry efforts. The first work is *Faith Coaching: A Conversational Approach to Helping Others Move Forward in Faith*, by Chad Hall, Bill Cooper, and Kathryn McElveen. Churches are slowly warming up to the idea of coaching in various ministries of the church, although the acceptance of this idea with children's ministry may be further behind than other ministries. Some might say, "Why would a children's ministry volunteer need a coach?"; however, this is not the right question to ask. A better question would be, "Why would a children's ministry volunteer not want a coach"?

As with any ministry, a coach could be a great source of encouragement and accountability to volunteers in the church. The coaching material can be focused on the spiritual development of individuals, which is something that every church should want for those serving in children's ministry. The authors describe what coaching is in the book and relay that coaching is all about relationship. This focus on relationships is left out of the development of ministry volunteers too often. Although almost every children's ministry has a point person, that individual cannot coach every member of the children's ministry team, even in smaller churches. This work focuses on how coaches should go about developing relationships and conversations that will lead individuals (or in this case volunteers) into a deeper walk with Christ.

The final work in this literature review comes from Dennis Williams and Kenneth Gangel who wrote *Volunteers for Today's Church: How to Recruit and Retain Workers*. Although an older work, this book (penned by Kenneth Gangel, a longtime Christian education professor at Dallas Theological Seminary) still provides valuable insight on ongoing recruitment and retention efforts in the local church. The book is filled with ideas on how to recruit and retain volunteers while tackling some of the problems churches often experience in this area.

If these simply stated principles were practiced, churches would recruit more effectively while reducing volunteer attrition in the local church. The authors touch on practices such as supervision, training, and communication that should be commonplace in the church but are often observed as lacking—thus contributing to attrition and a poor experience for someone who was called by God to serve an area of the church yet suddenly is bewildered and unenthused.

This scenario can be and should be avoided. Williams and Gangel show readers how to set up a system where volunteers do more than show up. They thrive in their role and look forward to continuing to serve because they feel part of something bigger than themselves that is making a difference for the kingdom.

Biblical Foundations

In Luke 2:52, the companion of the Apostle Paul states, "Jesus increased in wisdom and in stature and in favor with God and man." Although Jesus's circumstances were different, the only way that children will be able to develop into fully devoted Christ-followers is through other individuals who are influencing the life of a child. Although Mary and Joseph were instrumental in the development of Jesus, even He had interactions with others that defined him as a youngster.

With children, there is some truth to the saying, "It takes a village," in that many parents are unable to provide all the needed influence and encouragement to trigger a desire to follow Christ and seek after Him into adulthood. Most parents realize this and long for others (especially church leaders and volunteers) to partner with them. Churches that develop high-impact children's ministry volunteers are making a significant contribution to the spiritual development of the next generation.

If ever there was a time for children to be growing in wisdom, stature, and in favor with God and others, it is now. High-impact children's ministry volunteers play a great part in this growth through their service in the local church. Another passage that speaks to the value and honor that should be granted to ministry volunteers is Philippians 1:3–5. Here, Paul says, "I thank my God in all my remembrance of you, always in every prayer of mine for you all making my prayer with joy, because of your partnership in the gospel from the first day until now."

Paul had a unique understanding and view of those who served the local body. Paul was thankful to God for those who served at Philippi under the church leaders there. Paul did not create a list of names of those for whom he was thankful because he saw each who had committed themselves to serving the body of Christ as valuable. Interestingly, Paul avoided saying, "I want to thank all of you for your kingdom service;" he instead says, "I thank my God for you," possibly implying an even greater appreciation for their service. It is as if Paul was saying that there was no way his ministry would have been as fruitful had God not sent each person with his or her unique spiritual gifts to serve the church at Philippi.

The keyword in this passage as related to this project is the word, "Partnership," as Paul believed that each minister was important to the overall ministry of the church. The concept of partnership appears to be lost in today's church, as some gifts are elevated above others. There is no doubt that the senior pastor of a church is the head or should be the head of that local body, but the pastor must execute his ministry in a way that disguises this reality.

In other words, those individuals who are serving in children's ministry faithfully every week may never be heard by the masses and many may never know exactly what children's ministry volunteers do. Regardless, these individuals are key partners in the ministry and should be treated as such. We have already highlighted how God and Jesus esteem children; therefore, one can only imagine how He views the contributions of those who minister to children.

A third passage that is vital to understanding the need for equipping and training volunteers is Exodus 18:14–21. Moses, who was called by God as a volunteer leader of Israel, was facing burnout and disillusionment like many children's ministry volunteers and church volunteers in general. In this passage Moses says,

> When Moses's father-in-law saw all that he was doing for the people, he said, "What is this that you are doing for the people? Why do you sit alone, and all the people stand around you from morning till evening?" And Moses said to his father-in-law, "Because the people come to me to inquire of God; when they have a dispute, they come to me and I decide between one person and another, and I make them know the statutes of God and his laws." Moses's father-in-law said to him, "What you are doing is not good. You and the people with you will certainly wear yourselves out, for the thing is too heavy for you. You are not able to do it alone. Now obey my voice; I will give you advice, and God be with you! You shall represent the people before God and bring their

cases to God, and you shall warn them about the statutes and the laws, and make them know the way in which they must walk and what they must do. Moreover, look for able men from all the people, men who fear God, who are trustworthy and hate a bribe, and place such men over the people as chiefs of thousands, of hundreds, of fifties, and of tens.

Moses was struggling to provide appropriate leadership to the people of Israel and did not comprehend how to get the work of the ministry done without attempting to do it himself. The issue here, in part, is a staffing issue and, in part, an equipping issue for Moses. This also relates to empowerment as Moses had not appointed leaders beneath him for the task of ministry.

Due to this poor leadership model, Moses was burning out and it is likely other leaders close to him were as well. In this passage, several good things happened that allowed Moses to accomplish what God had called him to do. As Moses heeded the advice of Jethro, he began to recruit individuals with qualifications outlined by Jethro who could assist Moses:

> Moses' behavior is a model for modern-day leadership. We can see the priority he placed on the future by how he empowered younger leaders like Joshua. Simply put, leaders are responsible for future leadership. A leader who is not developing future leaders is not serving the organization well. The leader is either being shortsighted or selfish—shortsighted in that the future is not being considered or selfish in that the leader thinks only about himself/herself.[2]

As Jethro pointed out, these recruits would need to be men of skill and character in order for the tasks to be completed. Moses learned that he would have to trust his volunteers, and to survive, he would have to be content with letting go and letting volunteers do what God was calling them to do. Children's ministry volunteers are leaders in the church, and they need to consistently know that they are a part of the ministry team and that their service matters.

2. Geiger, "Leaving A Legacy of Leadership."

In the beginning of this passage, Moses appeared to have a difficult time grasping this concept, and for some churches, this problem continues to this day. Continuing to verse twenty-three in the same chapter, Jethro says to Moses, "If you do this, God will direct you, you will be able to endure, and all these people also will go to their place in peace."[3] This verse is important because as Moses followed the advice of Jethro, he did indeed survive. Even more, he ended up thriving as a leader.

Although Scripture does not explicitly say this, the volunteers were able to endure as well when Moses changed his leadership. Every volunteer needs clarity about what needs to be done and be empowered to do their work, these things happened in this passage. Every volunteer needs to know that their contribution matters and that they are a part of something bigger than themselves.

When changes were made, Moses' leadership was transformed, and those serving the Lord under him were energized for great work. This is very much commonsense leadership; yet, it so often fails to occur in churches to this day. The Israelites caught the vision that Moses was casting and worked toward reaching a common goal as a result of the change in perspective that he made with his volunteers that day.

Final Thoughts

The church has a gold mine of potential in the form of children attending weekly services and who are a part of a local body of believers. These are children who are growing up in the church and whose parents are laying the foundation for their kids to hear the gospel, accept Christ, and spiritually mature. However, more and more of these children are walking away from the faith, never to return. The church must become more intentional about embracing ministry opportunities to children by fully developing children's ministry volunteers who are not babysitters but who

---

3. Exodus 18:23.

have been called by God to spiritually impact the next generation through the gospel.

Every church has these individuals, and they long to see children come to saving faith and continue in their walk with Christ. The church also has a plethora of volunteers who want to make a difference in the lives of children and their families. Yet, like the children of Israel in the passage above, they often do not know what to do. There is minimal vision or a lack of connection to the vision, they are not equipped for the task, they are not empowered by church leaders, or they simply feel that although the church communicates a strong desire to minister to children they learn that this is not reality. These servants value children, see the potential in them just as Jesus did, and feel called to minister to them using the gifts and abilities God has given to them. The great American evangelist Dwight L. Moody stated, "If I could relive my life, I would devote my entire ministry to reaching children for God."[4]

There needs to be a revival of church leaders who will prioritize children's ministry and children's ministry leaders. It is time for the church to step up and engage its children's ministry volunteers in a way that expresses the urgency of the times. It is time for the church to reprioritize children and the volunteers who are working with them and their families. This reprioritizing will pay great dividends in reducing the scores of children who will later leave the church. Something must be done about this now, and it seems crucial that it begin with those children who are already in the fold and those children's ministry volunteers who have been called and empowered for this ministry.

---

4. Cacciolfli, *History of the Old Classic Children's Stories*, 14.

3

The Investigation

When it comes to children's ministry volunteerism in the church, some program approaches are viable, and others, not so much. Our research data points to the reality that many ministries across the United States are not well-managed nor focused regarding local church children's ministry volunteers. Our overall findings suggest that change is needed in how and why the church develops what may be its most important pool of volunteers. The following chapter focuses on the significance and implications of the survey results, which should stir readers to ruminate on how to improve upon their own current children's ministry volunteer structure. Even more, because children matter, it is quintessential to understand the deep social and cultural forces at play in the programs that surround the children in the church.

Survey Rationale

Two surveys were created to expose the lack of health in the development of church-based children's ministry volunteers. The data collected from the surveys was used to reveal the disparity between what those in pastoral leadership portray versus what those who are in the trenches serving children on a weekly basis in their local church experience. The results were expected to reveal a sharp contrast between the two parties mentioned above.

Specifically, the results revealed a measurable dissatisfaction among the children's ministry volunteers that will further reveal poor health and a low-impact children's ministry volunteer. The survey to ministry leaders reported a higher level of satisfaction with children's ministry volunteers and programs. The latter survey was expected to reveal happiness with the status quo regarding those serving in children's ministry and the weekly impact that volunteers are making in the lives and overall ministry of children in the church.

Survey Process

The first of the two surveys was designed in an attempt to capture data that would extract information that would reveal the activities that pastors and children's ministry leaders were doing to produce healthy, highly influential, children's ministry workers. We emailed the survey using SurveyMonkey.com to several senior pastors, all of whom were primarily located along the East Coast of the United States, ranging from New Hampshire to Florida.

Some pastors who participated led congregations that were established (well over one hundred years old) and would be considered megachurches due to their size, while other churches were church plants with less than five hundred in attendance and were less than five years old. As residents of the state of Virginia, the survey was also sent to pastors through the state convention of Southern Baptist Conservatives of Virginia (SBCV). A total of eight pastors contributed to the pastoral survey.

Participation was completely voluntary in all cases. Before sending the link to the survey, participants were sent an email with a consent form attached. The Institutional Review Board (IRB)[1] at Liberty University required the consent form be sent to all potential participants, but did not require it to be signed and returned. The consent form provided important contact information should the participants have any questions. The initial email that the survey was to gather data for a doctoral dissertation at Liberty University Baptist Theological Seminary surrounding the development of children's ministry volunteers in the local church. Participants were

1. See Appendix C.

selected because it was believed that their input into this research from their ministry would greatly benefit and enhance other local church children's ministries in their pursuit of high impact volunteers and healthy local church children's ministry.

Participants were also informed they would receive a subsequent email providing the link by which they could access the survey via SurveyMonkey.com's website. They were informed that the survey would be twenty questions and should take no more than fifteen minutes to complete. Their collected data would be submitted anonymously and in complete privacy. This pastoral survey was created and emailed to pastors in mid-December of 2013.

The second survey was emailed to potential participants in mid-January of 2014. There was minimal response from participants of the churches whose pastors had responded to the first survey. Due to the lower-than-expected response, we enlisted the assistance of the SBCV through one of its local state missionaries. The survey was sent out through the SBCV to every children's ministry worker who was in their database, or to over five hundred churches in the convention. Approximately twenty individuals responded to the survey, which was sent out through the SBCV. The total response to both surveys included eight pastors or senior children's ministry leaders and twenty-three children's ministry volunteers.

The second survey sought to compare the experiences of volunteers to what pastors had said they were doing for their children's ministry volunteers. We expected to discover multiple negative results of the comparison, but we were surprised that the overall experiences of volunteers revealed that they were committed to their service and seemed to be happily engaged in their ministry to children. Still, there were subtle signs pointing toward potential issues that could potentially derail the volunteer's service from a ministry standpoint.

There are a couple of reasons why we believe the volunteer survey results tilted more positively. First, many volunteers may have ignored the survey invitation due to their perceived belief that answering the questions would not change the circumstances surrounding their service. On the first survey, the pastors' responses were overwhelmingly positive, and this was due in part to the fact that most pastors are optimistic when discussing children's ministry.

Additionally, several of the pastors who participated in the survey were enjoying a high point in their respective ministries. The Spirit of God was moving, and individuals were coming to Christ in large numbers. Converts were being assimilated into the church in a healthy manner through baptism and church membership. Although there were obvious volunteer challenges in most ministries of the church, there was a growing wave of volunteers present who wished to serve and be a part of the body of Christ. The ministry excitement transferred into an eagerness to serve, which most likely translated to a positive experience for both pastor and volunteer.

Survey Question Overview

The first question addressed to children's ministry volunteers was multiple choice and defined what a healthy volunteer experience is and then asked participants whether or not they were having this type of experience. The question was multiple choice and sought to uncover the thoughts, feelings, and emotions of volunteers as related to their ministry. The choices were "Yes, I am," "No, I am not," "Not really sure," or "Other (please specify)." The last choice allowed for participant feedback.

The second question posed to volunteers was whether are not they could articulate the vision of the church. This is an important question that lends itself toward identifying a healthy volunteer. This was a yes-or-no question with another potential response of being able to articulate "a portion of the vision." If this question is not answered in the affirmative, there are potential pitfalls to the volunteer experience. Hopefully, the vision of the church incorporates the ministry to children so that there is an increased purpose behind the volunteers' ministry.

This led to the third question, which asked about whether the vision captured the value of children within it. Answer choices were "Yes," "No," "Not sure" or "Other (please specify)." Ministries whose volunteers answered, "Yes," were likely to have a healthy, positive atmosphere for children's ministry volunteers to thrive in their service.

Question four asked volunteers whether they felt their ministry to children helped to fulfill the vision of the church. This question was crafted in order to assess participants' knowledge and feelings about the ministry vision and whether or not there was a disconnect between knowing the ministry vision and whether or not the volunteer believed their service was fulfilling the vision. We believe that this is a key point of disconnection in many ministries: volunteers tend to reduce their level of service (or stop serving) because there is no vision or a lack of understanding about the vision that has been communicated by church leadership.

Question five asked volunteers about their children's ministry by inquiring, "Within your ministry as a children's ministry volunteer do you feel the church emphasizes the task more (changing the dirty diaper) or the ministry more (loving the child) as it relates to your service?" The rationale for asking this question was to gain information on how the volunteer felt he or she was being viewed by ministry leaders and even parents of children to whom the volunteers were ministering. If volunteer responses pointed toward emphasizing the task more than the ministry, then this could indicate a problem in the ministry.

Question five asked, "Do you believe current volunteer morale is high in the children's ministries of your church? If so, why? If not why?" The purpose of the question was to determine if there were differences in what volunteers believed about the children's ministry and what pastoral leadership would say about the same issue in a separate survey. After all, who has ever been to a church where a pastor would not provide high marks about the volunteers who serve children and families? Participants were allowed to provide feedback to this question.

Question seven asked volunteers, "Do you believe God has called you to serve in children's ministry?" The rationale for this question was to determine if there was a correlation between the call of God and volunteers persevering in children's ministry. The question also assists in determining whether the volunteer was perhaps coerced into accepting the volunteer position rather than serving because of being called by God to do so.

Question eight asked, "Do you believe your walk with Christ is growing stronger because of your service to the Lord as a children's ministry volunteer?" The purpose of this question was in part to assess whether volunteers were being challenged spiritually by ministry leaders and in part to gauge whether their children's ministry experience was contributing their spiritual growth.

Question nine asked, "Do you believe your church is invested in developing you as a children's ministry volunteer?" This question was asked because a church should design its volunteer ministry around building up the volunteer for the purpose of producing quality ministry through quality ministers. Unfortunately, this does not always happen.

Question ten asked volunteers, "Do you know your spiritual gifts and are they being utilized within your children's ministry role?" This question was asked because if a volunteer is ministering outside of their gifting, several things can jeopardize the impact of the volunteer's ministry. The volunteer could potentially burn out, frustration could set in, or the volunteer could become disillusioned with the ministry. On the other hand, if the volunteers know their spiritual gifts and are using them, they are more apt to be fulfilled in their role and calling because they are serving as they have been created.

Question eleven asked, "If you believed God was leading you to a different area of ministry within the church, do you feel there is freedom to explore this leading from God?" The rationale was to discover and gauge the health of the church and its volunteer ministry. A healthy church volunteer ministry will allow volunteers to explore other areas of the ministry as the Lord leads. An unhealthy ministry volunteer system or strategy will often lock in volunteers for extended periods, ignoring the feelings and even giftings of those volunteers.

Question twelve in the survey asked, "Do you believe the children's ministry leadership actively shows concern for your personal spiritual development through engagement, strategic planning, and accountability?" We believe that without the support of the senior leadership of the church, the effectiveness of the role of church volunteers is significantly reduced. All of the above areas are important and need attention in the life of the volunteer. If pastors are truly equipping the saints for ministry, then there must be a plan in place to ensure that this is occurring.

Question thirteen explored the question, "Are victories (wins) celebrated amongst volunteer children's ministry staff? If yes, how so?" The rationale for this question was to assess whether church leaders were celebrating victories with children's ministry volunteers. In other words, as God worked in the lives of children and families, how was this communicated or was there even communication to volunteers letting them know that God was using them to impact others in a powerful way?

Participant answers that were not in the affirmative could reveal several things, such as lack of vision and purpose. Failing to celebrate wins also reveals a lack of health and could lead to the volunteer burning out or losing focus on their God-ordained calling to reach children with the gospel.

Question fourteen was designed to complement question twelve but was more focused on pastoral leadership. The question asked, "As a volunteer do you feel supported by your Lead/Sr. Pastor and other pastoral staff members? If yes, how so?" We again wanted to assess whether volunteers felt that pastoral leadership in the church was truly partnering in their efforts to see children come to Christ through the delivery of excellent children's ministry programs.

Question fifteen sought to assess whether volunteers had been involved in recruiting for children's ministry. The questions asked, "Within the last year have you personally been involved in the successful recruiting of another children's ministry volunteer?" The rationale here was that a volunteer who recruits others themselves is a sign of a healthy ministry that has probably even benefited the volunteer. Volunteers who recruit others are most likely excited about their experience and desire others to join in with them. A volunteer who is not recruiting may, of course, be revealing the exact opposite.

Questions sixteen asked, "Do you feel the current training for children's ministry in your church is contributing to the development of healthy, high-impact children's volunteers?" This was another question designed to assess the level of support from the church. The level of training could at least in part reveal the level of impact volunteers were experiencing within their ministry. If best practices were not being offered and implemented into the children's ministry, this could potentially derail the overall health of this particular ministry and the spiritual experience for the children engaged in the ministry.

Question seventeen asked, "When serving the Lord in children's ministry, do you feel a strong sense that you are being prayed for or are being frequently lifted up in prayer by the church and church staff?" This is another question designed to gauge the most important part of spiritual support, which is essential to volunteer development and health. Since nothing of eternal significance happens apart from prayer, it is crucial that volunteers know that they are being lifted up to the Lord.

Question eighteen asked, "Which phrase best describes how you feel your ministry is viewed?" Response offerings were "I am a ministry volunteer," "I am a ministry partner," "I am just fulfilling a role," and "other." Although ministry volunteers should always be serving for an audience of one, it is still important that they, as well as others, view the volunteers of this ministry as ministry partners and nothing short of this.

Question nineteen provided participants a chance to share their thoughts. Participants were instructed, "Name 1 thing that you believe would enhance the health and overall impact of your church's children's ministry volunteer experience." We desired to hear from the volunteers as to what would be needed to improve the children's ministry volunteer experience. Twenty-one individual responses were made to this question. The question was asked to detect weak points or unhealthy aspects of a volunteer ministry experience.

The final question was asked to further probe areas of weakness within the volunteer ministry experience. The question asked, "What would you say is your greatest current frustration in serving as a children's ministry volunteer?" Twenty-two individual answers were provided, many of which offered clear points of frustration with the volunteer ministry experience. These responses assisted with understanding what many of the volunteers truly believe is the state of their ministry. Several of the survey questions were "Yes" or "No" format, which could allow a participant to escape expressing the reality of the current volunteer circumstances. The individual answers captured many areas of weakness and poor health within a church's volunteer systems and structure.

Survey Data

Individuals who chose to participate in the survey were able to access the survey by clicking on the link contained in the email. This link connected them to the customized survey on the SurveyMonkey website. All of the responses were collected through SurveyMonkey.com, which compiled the results that are presented in Table 2 and Table 3.

Table 2 shows the results of the volunteer survey.[2]

TABLE 2

Question[a]	Possible Responses	Results (%)
A healthy volunteer experience is one in which the volunteer displays passion about their service in a way that spiritually impacts others, while also bringing a sense of fulfillment to the volunteer. Are you currently having this type of experience as a volunteer in the children's ministry of your church?	Yes, I am	89.96
	No, I am not	4.35
	Not really sure	0.00
	Other (please specify)	8.70
Can you clearly articulate the vision of your church?[b]	Yes	90.91
	No	4.55
	I can articulate a portion of the vision	4.55
Do you believe the vision statement of the church incorporates the value of children somewhere in its message?	Yes	89.96
	No	4.35
	Not Sure	4.35
	Other	4.35
Do you believe your service to the Lord in children's ministry is fulfilling the vision of the church?	Yes	95.65
	No	4.35
	Not Sure	0.00
	Other	0.00
Within your ministry as a children's ministry volunteer do you feel the church emphasizes the task	Task More	13.04
	Ministry More	78.26

Figure 2: Volunteer Survey Responses

Table 3 reveals the results of the pastoral survey.[3]

TABLE 3

Question[a]	Possible Answers	Responses (%)
A healthy volunteer experience is one in which the volunteer displays passion about their service in a way that spiritually impacts others, while also bringing a sense of fulfillment to the volunteer. Do you believe your children's ministry volunteers are having a healthy experience serving in the children's ministries of your church?	Our children's ministry volunteers are having a healthy children's ministry volunteer experience.	62.50
	Our children's ministry volunteers are not currently enjoying a healthy volunteer children's ministry experience.	0.0
	I am unsure if our children's ministry volunteers are having a healthy volunteer experience.	0.0
	Other	37.5
Can children's ministry volunteers in your church clearly articulate the vision of the church?	All children's ministry volunteers can articulate the vision.	25.0
	Most children's ministry volunteers can articulate the vision of the church.	62.5
	Some of our children's ministry volunteers can articulate the vision of the church.	12.5

Figure 3: Pastoral/Ministry Leader Survey Responses

2. See Appendix D.
3. See Appendix E.

Survey Analysis

The surveys utilized in this book were conducted in the Fall of 2013. There were twenty-three responses from children's ministry volunteers and eight from pastors or those serving in children's ministry leadership for a combined total of thirty-one participants whose surveys have been analyzed. Survey results were mostly positive, which can be partially attributed to the fact that some of the churches surveyed were already experiencing success—meaning that some existing churches were going through a period of revitalization, while others were church plants that had experienced moves of God and great life change in their midst. We also believe that other survey participants were well supported in their ministry efforts by denominations such as the SBCV, as indicated by one survey participant, who expressed that denominational training had positively impacted the volunteer experience.

Healthy or Unhealthy Volunteers

An analysis of the data from the two surveys reveals some striking findings. We observed that for the majority of closed-ended questions volunteers and ministry leaders responded positively about their view of children's ministry volunteers or the importance of this ministry in their respective local church. It was as if when asked general questions, volunteers wanted to portray their church in a positive light and avoid being negative. Almost 90 percent of the volunteers surveyed indicated that they were experiencing a sense of fulfillment and impacting others with their service.

Additionally, some 87 percent of the volunteers surveyed indicated that their walk with Christ was growing in part due to their ministry service. Even with this high percentage of positive responses, one respondent reported not having a positive experience and two indicated in their responses to this question that they were progressing toward burnout, although they used the words "stressed" and "overwhelmed" in their responses.

Almost all of the children's ministry volunteers surveyed appeared to comprehend the basics of the ministry of the church, and a surprising 87 percent believed that the church vision incorporated children into the vision on some level. This was a very strong response, although the pastors surveyed responded with 100 percent affirmation to this question, indicating some gap, though not a large one. Furthermore, almost 80 percent of volunteers believed that their church was emphasizing the importance of ministry to children versus the many tasks involved in putting on a weekly children's ministry. This rate of positive response was even higher than pastors' and ministry leaders' beliefs on how their ministry viewed this topic.

When asked a multiple-choice question about morale with children's ministry volunteers, the pastors surveyed indicated that overall morale was good. Volunteers had the opportunity to write their responses to this question. Interestingly, the open-ended questions resulted in a more negative view of the experience. Some of the individual volunteer responses when asked if morale was high included "No. No one volunteers but me," "No, people don't want to teach children; they are more interested in the adult classes," "No, due to lack of leadership & training," and "I would say 50/50. Half love it; the other half do it because they feel they have to."

This part of the survey did not reveal the optimism that the results of many of the questions portrayed. The low morale of many volunteers indicates that some of the churches need to strengthen the volunteer culture in the church. As positive as many of the survey answers were, low morale will in time contribute to an unhealthy volunteer setting in which volunteers feel they are just doing a job each week, rather than engaging in life-changing ministry to children and their families.

In terms of training, the results were almost identical between pastors and volunteers. Seventy-five percent of pastors indicated that their church was investing heavily in children's ministry leadership development, and almost this same number of volunteers indicated that they believed their church was invested in their development. Over 91 percent of volunteers reported that they knew their gifts and they were using them through their ministry service to children.

There was, however, a disconnect as only 25 percent of the pastors surveyed indicated that they believed their church was providing ongoing training and development in the area of spiritual gifting with children's ministry volunteers. Perhaps a strong pulpit ministry explains the higher percentage of volunteers who appear to have grasped their gifts.

Another reason for the disparity may be the maturity level of the volunteers who were surveyed. It is possible that many of the volunteers had been equipped in this important aspect of ministry through their own personal study or through a previous church where they had served. With such a low percentage of pastors responding positively to this question, there is a possibility that volunteers were not receiving needed training in this area or they already knew their gifts and had no new needs to be learned.

The questions regarding training on the volunteer survey revealed that only 39 percent of the volunteers surveyed believed that the overall effort by their respective churches was adequate to develop healthy, high-impact children's ministry volunteers. However, some 63 percent of the pastors surveyed believed that the training provided was adequately developing healthy, high-impact children's ministry volunteers. Three of the pastors surveyed revealed that they were not sure if the training being provided was effectively equipping volunteers to truly make a difference for Christ.

Survey responses also revealed that 87 percent of volunteers felt called to children's ministry, and that the same percentage believed they were growing in their relationship with Christ. Additionally, some 88 percent of the pastors surveyed believed that those volunteering in children's ministry had a walk with Christ that was growing and were aided in this growth by their service to the Lord. The statistics here support the thought that despite the struggles and frustrations that some volunteers expressed in the written section of this survey, these volunteers are committed to the ministry to children (and their families) because they sense a call from God and they feel that their service assists them in drawing closer to Christ.

With both pastors and volunteers, the survey revealed a strong sense that there was a freedom to move to a different area of service within the church if the volunteer felt that calling. Some 91 percent of volunteers expressed that they believed they were free to experience other areas of the ministry. Ministry freedom represents a sign of a healthy volunteer culture. Any church or church staff that would restrict this movement is contributing to burnout and ministry dysfunction. The freedom to explore other ministries within the church was truly a welcomed observation from respondents.

Although volunteers who were surveyed felt supported as indicated previously, this was not the case when it came to engagement, accountability, and planning for the volunteers' spiritual development. Only 52 percent of surveyed volunteers felt that they were being provided these things from church leadership. Thankfully, for the churches represented, the volunteers apparently know how to feed themselves spiritually and take responsibility for their own development. Around 38 percent of the pastors surveyed acknowledged that their church made volunteers' spiritual development a priority.

This raises several questions. What if this were happening more with children's ministry volunteers? How much more productive would volunteers be? How much improved would the children's ministry experience be for everyone involved? If volunteers are left to themselves with little to no accountability as this indicates, it is amazing that there are not more issues of dysfunction and burnout amongst volunteers.

The survey statistics reveal some issues with recruiting volunteers. Ideally, a ministry would see most new children's ministry volunteer recruitment coming through a contagious word-of-mouth excitement from current children's ministry volunteers. Surveys within this research indicated that only about 64 percent of volunteers had successfully recruited another volunteer to serve in children's ministry.

THE INVESTIGATION

According to the pastoral survey, this important aspect of ministry was executed more by church staff than by the volunteers. Some 75 percent of church senior leadership responded that they were most responsible for the ongoing drive to recruit children's ministry volunteers. In some churches, this may be the system in place, but one could argue that volunteers recruiting volunteers is a sign of health in terms of the culture and work of God in a particular ministry.

Encouraging volunteers to recruit other volunteers allows current volunteers to share what God is doing in the ministry as well as in their own lives. If volunteers are truly excited about the ministry, they will almost always make recruitment efforts, but if they are not making an effort to recruit, then then the opposite would be true. A good balance of staff and volunteers recruiting volunteers may be an even better approach.

One pastor commented on his survey:

> It is a team effort between staff and volunteer leaders. We have semi-annual church-wide volunteer "pushes" that are driven from the stage and managed by the staff, as well as ongoing monthly Volunteer Orientation meetings which recruit a portion of our volunteers. However, our volunteer leaders and volunteers are constantly recruiting in a "grass roots" way and bringing more people into their teams that way. Many times, recruiting will happen in conversations with a parent at drop off or pick up, or just among the children's ministry volunteers' circle of friends and family. There is a lot of camaraderie among the teams and that is very inviting for others who see it in action.

If recruiting is accomplished as mentioned here, the ministry and the volunteer benefit because the ministry engages a new volunteer into service and the volunteer involved in the recruiting gets to see how God is using them to build the ministry.

Another important aspect of volunteer ministry is the language leaders use in communicating with volunteers. Half of pastors and ministry leaders surveyed indicated that their children's ministry volunteers were just "volunteers." One of the choices on this question on the survey was to describe the volunteer as a "ministry partner," and only 25 percent of ministry leaders viewed children's ministry volunteers this way. Nearly 61 percent of the volunteers did view themselves as a "ministry partner," which, in comparison, is good, but the results do not adequately esteem individuals who are serving children's ministry or any other ministry for that matter or define them as partners in ministry.

Reducing a servant of God to something below a partner in ministry truly is revealing. This reduction of the volunteer may have happened innocently, but it may also signal that the church is more staff driven than lay driven. Treating volunteers as "ministry partners" is what is portrayed in Scripture and needs to be modeled in churches, today. If one were to compare a volunteer who only felt he or she was a "volunteer" with one who believed he or she was a "ministry partner," one would most likely see a difference in how that person viewed their service (and in the passion and excellence they displayed in their ministry).

When asked about what would enhance the children's ministry of the church, some of the pastors commented with the following: (a) "More support from senior pastor," (b) "More friendship among serving volunteers," (c) "More training," (d) "A more strategic training and continual learning process," (e) "More structure in the programs," (f) "Increased/better vision casting for the 'why behind the what' and the importance of children's ministry," (g) "More training specific for children's ministry. But this would need to be done at times that minimally impact their home life," and (h) "More volunteers rising up to lead. As we grow, this naturally is our biggest need in all of our ministry areas."

Children's ministry volunteers responded to a similar question by stating, "If more people would volunteer and if I had more resources to build a better program," "If more of my brothers and sisters in Christ would spend more time praying about serving and seeking the Lord's direction by spending more personal daily quiet time in the Bible," "Having more volunteer to lessen the burden on the" faithful few," "If volunteers could realize how important this job is and how they can impact a child's life when there is so much dysfunction among families now," "Prayer," "Meeting together to pray and talk about our mission for the evening," "More team players," and "Clearly defined roles and responsibilities." Three volunteers indicated that more ministry training would be useful.

These answers clearly indicate that there are volunteers who are struggling in most children's ministry programs. There is clearly a need for improved training, more prayer among clergy and volunteers, more vision-casting so that roles are defined and that volunteers understand the why behind the ministry, and finally for more ongoing support and resources to be dedicated to children's ministries.

When asked, "What is the greatest current frustration with anything related to children's ministry volunteers in your church?" pastors responded with the following: "Commitment level," "The only thing that comes close to the word frustration is the idea that all ministries should be viewed equally important. Often this is not the case," "Lack of volunteers," "Not having enough volunteers/competing with other ministries," "Always recruitment of more workers," and "We are in need of more servants in our kids' ministry."

On the pastoral side of the survey, the overriding theme is that there just needs to be more volunteers serving in children's ministry. Frustrations mentioned from volunteers included comments such as "Feeling like I am the only one who is trying to make the ministry exciting and fresh. Too many seeing it as 'Another church job and not ministry,'" "Not being engaged by the church leader(s)," "Getting people to commit to a regular service schedule," "Need more ministry partners," "That more people do not see the value and satisfaction of reaching these kids for Christ and get on board," "Keeping good volunteers," "As a group we show up at different times, give our lessons and leave whenever. I don't feel as though I am working as a team with the others," "Some adults don't understand the importance of our ministry, what we're doing and why," "Volunteers not showing up for their time on duty," "Lack of vision of parents and families, not following through on what a church day has been in their child's life" and "Too many volunteers don't believe it is a much needed ministry that allows parents a chance to worship."

As alluded to earlier, many of the ministry volunteers who were surveyed appear to be in healthier churches where staff and volunteers are striving to truly make a difference in the lives of children by empowering committed ministry partners. There are, of course, many who did not participate in this survey who are leaving children's ministry because of the lack of support and personal development. They are most likely in a much less healthy ministry setting than many of the volunteers and pastors surveyed for this project. There is no doubt that both pastors and volunteers could use a ministry plan to develop a healthier base of engaged children's ministry volunteers to meet the needs of the local church.

What if both ministry leaders and volunteers were speaking the same ministry language and had the same goals for children's ministry? What if every volunteer knew their roles and expectations for ministry? What if there was so much excitement in the church about ministering to children that there was never a shortage of ministry partners and volunteers? What if both ministry leaders and ministry partners felt supported by the senior leadership of the church? What if every ministry partner and local church member truly understood the vision of the church and the important place children have within both the local body and the universal church?

In short, there are mixed results regarding children's ministry healthiness represented in our findings. There are some things that could be celebrated within the findings and several items that need to be addressed and improved. A plan is needed for changes to take place as they will not occur on their own. Churches need strategic assistance in developing healthy, high-impact children's ministry volunteers. Children matter to God, and if they matter to God, they must be a part of the foundational mission of every local church.

4

The Discussion

The question remains whether pastors and leaders have a system in place for the development of children's ministry volunteers in the church. The days of "Go see sister Sally or brother Joe and they will help you get plugged in" have ended for ministry volunteers. With time constraints and minimal energy left in people's emotional tanks by the end of the week, most ministry volunteers will simply choose not to serve if they sense that the church has not been proactive in developing a clearly defined system that includes training for their development.

Some of the key things our research revealed were that volunteers wanted to see these development components in place, they longed to be coached, and that they desired clarity regarding their ministry roles. They may not have overtly proclaimed, "I want a system, coaching, clarity, or training," but the fine details revealed in their answers clearly pointed to this as being a key factor. Thus, because children matter, it is important to hear the hearts and concerns of children's ministry volunteers.

Concepts to Ponder

Every church should be known as a place where any child who participates finds themselves engaging in a vibrant ministry experience provided by trained members of the body of Christ. They will eventually leave different but improved—as in closer to God and better equipped to either become more like Christ or to come to know Him as personal Lord and Savior. These children deserve to be ministered to by a volunteer who is passionate about children and passionate about ministering to children.

Unfortunately, many children who will attend church this coming Sunday will for multiple reasons not discover the children's ministry volunteer described above, and more importantly, they will possibly leave church with their spiritual needs unmet, when they perhaps could have been met if the church and its children's ministry volunteers were prepared for ministry on this day. There is simply too much at stake for this to continue occurring. There is too short of a window of opportunity for the church to not capitalize on the opportunity.

Therefore, based on the findings presented from the surveys in chapter 3, several strategies will be prescribed. These approaches can assist churches in the development of children's ministry volunteers who are serious and who truly seek to minister in such a way in which God is glorified and that children (and their families) are drawn closer to God each week in the children's ministry.

Children's Ministry Volunteers' Need for a System

The lack of a ministry system was not overtly revealed as a negative aspect of the survey data, but there were some comments made by volunteers within the surveys that indicated a system would be beneficial for those serving in children's ministry. Approximately 80–90 percent of performance issues are not related to an individual but to poorly implemented systems.[1] Too many ministries operate as if there is a looming emergency when a deeper look reveals poor planning or the lack of a system in place to develop volunteers.

Comments from research participants indicated a lack of morale for several reasons, including that almost 30 percent of volunteers mentioned they would like to be developed more and that only 39 percent of volunteers believed in the effectiveness of the current level of training for children's ministry volunteers. It

---

1. Gerson, *Achieving High Performance*, 46.

THE DISCUSSION

is evident that a development system for volunteers is needed in every church. Nelson Searcy defines a system as "any ongoing process that saves you stress, time, energy, and money, and continues to produce results."[2] Testimonies are available from many who are stressed and on the verge of ministry burnout because there is no system in place to develop and equip ministry volunteers in a way that will bring about ministry success.

Typically, ministries that have a system in place for their volunteers have volunteers who are engaged and who enjoy a fulfilling ministry experience that benefits those they are serving. Eisner (referring to a national workforce study) indicated, "The study concludes that fewer than half of nonprofits that manage volunteers have adopted a significant number of important volunteer management practices."[3]

According to Searcy, "Good structure helps people see how they fit into the overall ministry and how their roles relate to others. Problems arise when this is not clear. Individuals and groups go in different directions, and chaos replaces harmony."[4] Searcy goes on to say, "The ministry system is an ongoing system that motivates people to serve for the first time and mobilizes them for a lifetime of serving."[5]

The organization that a church puts in place needs to address some of the very things survey respondents mentioned in this research. A system must address volunteer support to include coaching and structure, ministry clarity, volunteer community, ministry vision, and volunteer care. Flanagan mentions,

> A critical component of an effective ministry is its ability to be organized. The organizational responsibilities rest upon the shoulders of the leadership. If it is perceived that the ministry is not organized, volunteers will not be likely to follow the leader. Conversely, when the leader organizes ministries in order to accomplish a task, those

2. Searcy and Henson, *Connect*, 32.
3. Eisner et al., "New Volunteer Workforce."
4. Searcy and Henson, *Connect*, 34.
5. Searcy and Henson, *Connect*, 34.

who serve alongside the leader are more apt to follow. Further, the ministry that is organized is more likely to accomplish its purpose. Disorganized ministries experience no growth, expansion, or innovation.[6]

The place to begin with developing a system for children's ministry volunteers would be to assess the current system that is in place for volunteers. Having no system in place would still constitute having a system. For example, if a church just allows whoever shows up to minister to children, this demonstrates the system that is currently in place, albeit a flawed one. Some time would need to be taken to assess some of the following:

1. How are children's ministry volunteers currently recruited? Where is the entry point for a volunteer to begin serving in children's ministry?

2. How are children's ministry volunteers currently receiving the vision for children's ministry?

3. How are children's ministry volunteers currently encouraged and developed?

4. How are children's ministry volunteers currently supported by senior members of church leadership?

5. How are children's ministry volunteers currently being cared for by the church?

6. How much of the church budget is devoted to children's ministry volunteer development?

7. How many children's ministry volunteers currently receive coaching?

8. How are children's ministry volunteers currently celebrated within the church? Is there a yearly banquet or a volunteer of the month?

9. How are children's ministry volunteers currently being evaluated? Is there ever a review?

---

6. Flanagan, *Successful Volunteer Organization*, 129.

10. How many lives have been changed as a result of the ministry provided by children's ministry volunteers?

Although the aforementioned are not an exhaustive list that a church can use to discern the current state of its volunteer ministry to children, these are solid questions to begin the process. If a system is in place, one would also need to determine how complicated the current system is. If recruiting, for example, is an issue, then perhaps the steps toward volunteering are confusing or there is no designated point person to discuss opportunities for serving in children's ministry. Should this be the case, the church needs to make revisions to the system that is in place. Craig Larson states,

> The point is, we need to think systems, build systems, and put people in charge of systems. And we also need to monitor their health. If there is a problem, we must ask the Lord what systems are needed to correct it. Systems are tributaries feeding into the whole church process.[7]

Larson's statement describes the reason so many churches struggle to find capable volunteers to serve children and with other ministries of the church. There is simply no ministry network in place (or the one in place is broken). There has to be a system in place in order for there to be sustained health and growth of volunteers.

Nelson Searcy says, "We may not be aware of a good system when it is running well, but there is no mistaking when something isn't working like it should."[8] What seems to plague many churches is with no official, orchestrated system in place, there is great difficulty in fixing issues that affect children's volunteer ministries. Failing to develop volunteer support for ministry is failing the children who will be ministered to, failing the volunteer because of the frustration that is often created, and, one could say, failing biblically.

Searcy goes on to say,

---

7. Brown and Larson, *Other Side*, 96.
8. Searcy, *Healthy Systems*, Location 293.

Paul understood God's affinity for systems. That's why, in trying to help us wrap our minds around how the church should function, he compared the body of Christ to the human body. He aligned the design of the church with the functioning of our own different parts. In Romans, Paul writes, "Just as each of us has one body with many members, and these members do not all have the same function, so in Christ we who are many form one body, and each member belongs to all the others." Sounds remarkably like how God designed our physical bodies with systems, right? Go back and read the verse again substituting the word, "systems," every time you see the word "members." Makes perfect sense, doesn't it?[9]

The purpose of this section is not to outline an exact system that will develop incredible children's ministry volunteers, but to mention the many benefits of having such a system in place. Every church is different, so outlining one system that fits them all is impossible. Every church needs to take the time to evaluate what is currently in place and then work toward developing a system that honors God and communicates to children's ministry volunteers that their service and the ministry to children is a high priority.

We believe that some of the comments made by survey participants may not have been made if an adequate system was in place that had developed children's ministry volunteers, appropriately. Searcy further states, "Your system is designed to give you exactly what it is giving you."[10] It seems that many churches do not have enough volunteers to effectively staff a children's ministry. Many volunteers expressed at least some frustration in the survey. Pastors also sounded in with remarks that were less than positive about what was taking place with children's ministry volunteers.

Perhaps there is a lack of organization in the church that is leading to confusion, burnout, and lack of production from children's ministry volunteers. The questions previously mentioned are a good starting point for assessing the state of ministry volunteers. This may mean spending some time at length

---

9. Searcy, *Healthy Systems*, Location 79.
10. Searcy, *Healthy Systems*, Location 99.

THE DISCUSSION

as a ministry staff (including children's ministry volunteers) and working toward building a long-term system that will energize children's ministry volunteers. Ultimately, this will allow them to focus more exclusively on being able to minister to children and their families each week.

In addition to the previously mentioned questions, Searcy offers four additional questions to assess the state of volunteerism for evaluating the state of children's ministry volunteerism. These include questions such as 1) how many passionate volunteers do you have, 2) how many passionate volunteers would you like to have, 3) what are you doing to make people want to serve, and 4) when was the last time you personally invested in your volunteers?[11]

Those churches that are financially able might want to consider an outside consulting firm such as Ministry Architects to do an in-depth analysis of all the components of the current children's ministry so that a system or revitalized system can be developed to strengthen the children's ministry and the volunteers who serve in it.

Children's Ministry Volunteers' Need for Coaching

"Coaches for children's ministry volunteers?" one might question. Some may be astounded at the notion because it is so rare. A better question might be, "Why not coaches for children's ministry volunteers?" Ecclesiastes 4:9–12 states,

> Two are better than one, because they have a good return for their labor: If either of them falls down, one can help the other up. But pity anyone who falls and has no one to help them up. Also, if two lie down together, they will keep warm. But how can one keep warm alone? Though one may be overpowered, two can defend themselves. A cord of three strands is not quickly broken.

---

11. Searcy, *Healthy Systems,* Location 99.

The church has been slower to warm to the coaching model than the business world, but many now see the importance of it, primarily in areas such as small group ministry. Pastor Matt Wilmington of Thomas Road Baptist Church spoke to the need for coaching volunteers when he said,

> If I spend my energy creating a culture of serving and connect people to ministry, but never train and encourage them in their jobs, I am sending the slave-vision message—"I just want you working; I don't really care about you." Not only that, but if I am unleashing an untrained army in my church and on my community, someone is going to get hurt! There will be spiritual malpractice and personal burnout because my volunteers simply do not know what they are doing. Coaching, then, is a critical component of leadership. It moves us from leading people into ministry, to leading people in their ministry.[12]

The need for coaching is due to the need for ministry support. The research indicated, in part, that volunteers would like to have more support. There is no better way to support a children's ministry volunteer than by providing them with a coach to help guide, encourage, train, counsel, and pray for the volunteer. Coaching is also more of a team-approach to ministry, and in most cases, teams can go further than individuals, as supported by Ecclesiastes 4:9–12.

The answers from volunteers in our research indicated that less than 55 percent of volunteers believed that they were being prayed for by someone in the church or by church staff, and only 61 percent of volunteers believed they were a ministry partner in their service to their church. Individual participants mentioned some requests when asked to name one thing that would enhance the overall impact of their children's ministry experience. Some of the responses were, "For the volunteers to make themselves available for the training that is offered. We've even sent links to them to do on their own and some do not open them," "meeting together

---

12. Falwell, *InnovateChurch*, 53.

THE DISCUSSION

to pray and talk about our mission for the evening," "prayer," and "clearly defined roles and responsibilities."

These answers indicate that there is a need for coaching amongst the volunteers who were surveyed. If a coach had been in place, it is likely that these comments would not have been shared because those spiritual needs would have already been met. Children's ministry volunteers are leaders in their respective churches, and

> when leadership works well, it is a marvelous thing. And when it doesn't people are damaged. You have been given a great privilege if you are a leader—whether in an organization, a church, a school, a business, or even in a family. People are desperately looking for guidance. They need to come under good influences.[13]

The following aphorism is still quite true today: people, especially volunteers, are looking for guidance. They are often not the decision makers and may not be informed like a paid staff person would be. They deserve to be sharpened, challenged, and informed about all that their ministry role entails.

A children's ministry coach would have the opportunity to inform, pray with, and strategize with volunteers about this important ministry calling and role. The coach fulfilling this role should be one who is already serving in children's ministry or who has served faithfully in this role in the past. Someone spiritually mature and a veteran in this ministry arena would be ideal. Coaching is most effective when the volunteer realizes that they truly need it to be most effective. Every team member needs an outside source at times to stimulate them in order to thrive and be built up as an individual and a unit.[14]

If those serving in children's ministry are not being built up and strengthened for the ministry ahead, it is difficult to expect long-term results and productivity from the volunteer. Bob Nelson states, "You get the best results from others not by lighting

---

13. Lawrenz, *Spiritual Influence*, 27.
14. Cloud, *Power of the Other*, 151.

a fire beneath them, but by building a fire within."[15] As part of building up the volunteer in a coaching session, the right kinds of questions need to be asked.

A conversation model has been offered by Hancox, Hunter, and Boudreau to help guide coaches of volunteers. This model has the potential to elevate volunteer engagement, which will empower the volunteer for greater ministry to children and their families. More than anything, coaching, using the road map provided, would speak volumes to the volunteer about the importance of their ministry and many new and innovative ideas to further the ministry would evolve from these conversations.

The model assists coaches with building self-awareness and energy management while providing tips for feedback, appreciative discovery and heightened engagement.[16] If every children's ministry had a coach who would follow this model, it would be astounding to see the effects of this type of personal touch and concern for the volunteer. This coaching road map would build several things into the life of the volunteer. As Stoltzfus stated, "We need support, encouragement and accountability to function at our full capacity. That's why leaders with a coach get more done."[17]

One may wonder if coaching is really necessary in children's ministry. This doubt could be one of the more difficult parts of beginning coaching children's ministry volunteers: that there will be some who do not understand the need for coaching. If this doubt is mouthed in a local church, as it probably will be in some, a greater level of dysfunction would be revealed, in that the children's ministry volunteer role has been lowered to a disgraceful level.

Both the Apostle Paul and Jesus Christ were examples of what good coaching can do for someone who is serving. The Apostle Paul and Jesus both believed in the people they came in contact with. They wanted the best for those individuals who walked beside them; often this involved walking with individuals through

15. Hancox et al., *Coaching for Engagement*, 125.
16. Hancox et al., *Coaching for Engagement*, 42.
17. Stoltzfus, *Leadership Coaching*, 38.

challenging circumstances. Tony Stoltzfus, speaking of Jesus impact on the early church, said,

> The first leaders of the early church came from the group of those who bore responsibility with him, not the crowds who heard him speak from a distance. You can develop leaders in the same way Jesus did: give them responsibility and then walk with them as they carry it out. Coaching provides the tools and the structure you need to do a great job of raising up leaders.[18]

When considering the coaching model previously described, it is apparent that Jesus coached using many of the techniques mentioned. Jesus was a master of building self-awareness in his volunteers, and He primarily did this through listening skills and the asking of powerful questions. Jesus assisted with the development of talents while confirming the strengths of His followers. This led to a level of heightened engagement, which allowed the Disciples to go out and change the world. As a final step of personal coaching, one could say that Jesus provided the disciples with the next steps to take before He ascended into heaven, in the form of the Great Commission.

If a church is struggling in the area of children's ministry volunteer development, one cause could be the failure to use a coaching system for volunteers. It is difficult to find a better way for volunteers to thrive and develop their full potential in ministry apart from having a coach. Children's ministry volunteers who are under the guidance of a qualified ministry coach will go further in their ministry and develop faster as a result of good coaching. The business world sees the value a coach brings to the table, and the sports world certainly sees the value. Perhaps it is time for the church to recognize that the volunteers who serve the most precious commodity in the church (children) deserve the opportunity to be coached and developed in the most professional way possible.

D. B. Huesser remarked, "A great deal of the volunteer's response, whether positive or negative, has to do with the help,

---

18. Stoltzfus, *Leadership Coaching*, 44.

direction, assistance, encouragement, and support that the volunteer receives."[19] This support almost never comes from the senior pastor, and there is nothing wrong with this, although the senior pastor needs to be the champion of children's ministry and its volunteer servants. Because a pastoral team member is usually not able to fulfill this role, having a trained children's ministry coach assigned to a volunteer will serve to propel the volunteer toward greater service, which will surely impact the children's ministry in a positive way.

The more support the children's ministry volunteers can be provided, the more likely volunteers are to serve at a high level and embrace the opportunity that has been provided to them. Without a coaching structure, it is most likely a matter of time before there will be children's ministry volunteers leaving this area of the ministry. A coach plays a vital role in not only providing encouragement and prayer but of keeping the vision before the volunteer. This is key as volunteers need to continually hear why they are serving.

Children's Ministry Volunteers' Need for Clarity

When survey participants were asked what would be one thing that would enhance the impact of the church's children's ministry volunteer experience, a few remarked on the need for increased ministry clarity. Some of the comments included, "If more people would volunteer and if I had more resources to build a better program," "Need more volunteers to ensure enough coverage," "If volunteers could realize how important this job is and how they can impact a child's life when there is so much dysfunction among families now," "clearly defined roles and responsibilities" and "meeting together to pray and talk about our mission for the evening."

Lack of ministry clarity negatively affects many aspects of ministry, from recruiting and training to understanding ministry roles and responsibilities. If potential workers discern a lack of clarity in a church's children's ministry, they are unlikely to want to join

---

19. Heusser, *Helping Church Workers Succeed*, 19.

this ministry. Eric Geiger says, "Clarity is the ability of the process to be communicated and understood by the people . . . If you want your process to be clear, you must define it, illustrate it, discuss it, and measure it. You must also constantly monitor the understanding of your people in regard to your process."[20]

If the current volunteers begin to discern a lack of clarity surrounding their purpose and vision for ministry, why would they want to continue serving? Furthermore, the children and families being served could begin to sense that the ministry that is being conducted is not necessarily being done in a way that has the best in mind for the children and those serving as volunteers. In other words, without clarity of vision and purpose, there is a slow ministry death that takes place—slow, as in this process could take years, but the decline begins to show itself in the form of reduced numbers of children, reduced numbers of volunteers, reduced enthusiasm for the ministry, and reduced quality of programming.

With this in mind, most churches operate just as Simon Sinek describes in his book, *Start With Why*. He writes, "When most organizations or people think, act or communicate they do so from the outside in, from what to why. And for good reason—they go from clearest thing to the fuzziest thing. We say what we do, we sometimes say how we do it, but we rarely say why we do what we do."[21]

Children's ministry volunteers rarely get the "Why" that Sinek mentions here, but the "Why" is something that needs to be clear and repeated often. Volunteers need to know why they are serving as they have been asked to serve. They need to know how their role plays out in terms of the overall ministry of the local church in which they serve. Sinek goes on to say,

> Knowing your why is not the only way to be successful, but it is the only way to maintain a lasting success and gave a greater blend of innovation and flexibility. When a why goes fuzzy, it becomes much more difficult to

---

20. Rainer and Geiger, *Simple Church*, 111.
21. Sinek, *Start with Why*, 39.

maintain the growth, loyalty and inspiration that helped drive the original success.[22]

Clarity is also extremely important to the church or organization because whether the church or organization realizes it or not, they are dependent on the volunteers for this "greater blend of innovation and flexibility" mentioned by Sinek that every church or organization needs to move forward. Although church staff typically sets this course in many ways, if there is ongoing clarity of vision taking place, volunteers will often lead the way to becoming more innovative. Lack of clarity hinders organization innovation, as Sinek has mentioned. Lack of understanding among team members concerning the mission and core values will often lead to team members taking matters into their own hands, which is almost always frustrating for team members. Having a built-in structure creates an atmosphere in which team members can thrive and strengths can be developed.[23]

The word, thrive, is an important word because children's ministry volunteers want to thrive. This is one of the likely reasons they initially accept the volunteer role. Not only do they want to thrive, but they want the children to whom they minister to thrive as well.

To thrive is to have clarity; it is difficult to thrive in any setting without having clarity of purpose and values. With this said, clarity is almost always something that a leader will need to provide to volunteers. Whoever is leading the ministry to children at the church—along with the senior pastor—will continuously need to be working to provide clarity to the ministry in the form of vision, core values, roles, and expectations.

The volunteer's primary role is to be able to communicate with clarity to anyone who may ask what the vision, core values, roles, and expectations are. It is problematic in many ways and reveals a lack of knowledge and clarity concerning the vision if volunteers are unable to clearly communicate this to others. The

---

22. Sinek, *Start with Why*, 50.
23. Adams, *Children's Ministry on Purpose*, 159.

THE DISCUSSION

goal should be for every volunteer to be able to verbalize these concepts. If a visitor comes to a church and asks five different children's ministry volunteers about the mission of children's ministry within the church, they should only receive one answer to their question—not five answers.

Those who might ask would include parents, volunteers in other areas of ministry, and maybe even the children who are being served. The leader needs to bring clarity to the ministry, and the volunteer needs to be able to communicate what they have received with clarity. Clarity is only achieved when there is a clear understanding of the ministry direction by all parties involved. Anything less than this will bring a level of complexity that can stifle the volunteer as well as the ministry itself. This does occur at times, but when it does, immediate steps need to be taken to correct this problem.

Failure to do so in a timely manner could lead to the demise of the ministry and eventual loss of the volunteer's services. With the above point made here, one thing that would be helpful is regular debriefing sessions with children's ministry volunteers after volunteers have engaged in a serving opportunity. Bill Hybels states, "If volunteers say they loved every minute of the experience, we can just cheer them on and encourage them to continue. If they express reservations about going back, we need to find out why."[24]

A recommendation would be for leaders to have four to six debriefings a year or to debrief after major children's event on the church calendar, such as a fall festival or vacation Bible school. This would allow the children's ministry pastor or children's director to ask important questions to be sure that the mission and goals that were hopefully presented for the ministry were accomplished. If the "Win" of the ministry was clarified before the event, it might help avoiding or alleviating with unavoidable problems or issues.

There also could have been a move of God in a way that no one saw coming before the event, which may mean the "Win" for the next ministry would change or be reframed. The ministry will move forward in a more productive and organized way as a result

---

24. Hybels, *Volunteer Revolution*, 112.

of debriefings with children's ministry volunteers. Furthermore, children's ministry volunteers will value the opportunity to provide feedback and appreciate the fact that a ministry leader was interested enough to hear their feedback on the ministry that took place. This is simply an optimum situation for the church and the ministry that was provided.

Bridging the Clarity Gaps

William Mancini provides insights into how easy it is for clarity to be lost. Bringing ministry clarity to the vision and mission of a group of children's ministry volunteers is much more than simply spouting words. The leader may perceive one thing, while the volunteer perceives something totally different. Bridging the clarity gap involves relational connection, patience, and a willingness to pursue feedback from individuals. Between the effort of the leader to provide clarity and with their personal investment, there is a strong likelihood that clarity gaps can be avoided.[25]

Clarity gaps in children's ministry could arise if church leadership does not take the time to invest in children's ministry workers relationally. An example of this could be if there were multiple behavioral issues present among the "Sparks" group of children at Wednesday night A.W.A.N.A. Volunteers become frustrated due to the ongoing behavioral issues and they communicate this frustration to the church staff.

Despite having the issue communicated to them, church staff perceive that everything in children's ministry is going well. For whatever reason, the choice is made to ignore a glaring problem that is affecting children and volunteers, thereby lowering the morale of the program. This intentional (or unintentional) misperception of ministry health fogs the clarity of the vision for the children's program. The lack of awareness of reality can lead to a possible lack of clarity for volunteers, which could lead some volunteers to question why they are doing what they are doing.

25. Mancini, *Church Unique*, 57.

THE DISCUSSION

One type of clarity gap involves the leaders' words in comparison to how they are being interpreted by followers. This is sometimes visible in ministries that might attempt to do ministry on a whim and do not plan appropriately at times. The leader of children's ministry volunteers needs to be careful that they are communicating in a way that allows everyone to leave meetings in one accord.

For example, if the children's ministry leader tells volunteers that the children's ministry is committed to reaching every child in the community for Christ, but only states that certain children will not be allowed to participate in an activity, then the message has become convoluted. There is now lack of clarity and confusion about the purpose of the children's ministry. There is also the possibility that many people have been offended with the additional possibility of discouragement due to a misunderstanding of the mission that has now been birthed in the minds of volunteers.

Children's ministry leadership has to be careful with the words that they use to communicate the mission and core values because if one thing is quoted but misunderstood by followers, an entire season of ministry could be lost. Children's ministry leadership must be as relational as they can with volunteers in order for volunteers to gain the clarity that they need.

Hans Finzel provided several tips to help with leaders provide excellent ministry clarity. Have face time with your leaders. Play and pray with those you lead. Schedule regular off-site meetings for team development that include play as well as work. Make internal communications a top priority of your job. Keep your followers informed as to what you expect of them. Find ways to articulate and communicate vision and values. Make sure that formal communication systems are in place. Avoid the great surprise. Do not ambush people who are not doing their jobs well. Be honest. "MbWA," a.k.a., "Manage by Wandering Around." Get out of your office, but be sensitive to others achieving their goals/do not interrupt another's workflow. Find ways to tap into the underground within your organization. Have informants. Practice "HOT" communication—e.g., be "Honest, Open, and Transparent." Finally, nothing happens until people talk.[26]

Attempts should be made to secure regular feedback from volunteers to be sure that their voice on matters related to children's ministry is being heard. A quarterly survey for children's ministry volunteers would be a good starting place and can be used to monitor the language being used by leadership to ensure that there is clarity of mission and purpose. Leaders could even use short vignettes once a month that could be emailed to further clarify the vision for children's ministry and volunteers.

Stanley provides the following imagery concerning the importance of ministry clarity:

> Imagine the advantage you would have if everyone in your church operated on the same internal code. What if every volunteer and every staff member understood that certain practices were critical to the success of your mission, and that these practices were an essential part of the style and culture of your ministry? Now, what if you could somehow shape these principles into words and phrases that could be effectively integrated into the language of your ministry—simple statements that would instantly remind the players on your team how and why they do what they do?[27]

Some awesome questions were asked by Stanley. What if every volunteer had the same internal code regarding children's ministry? With modern-day technological advances, there is no excuse for ministries in any church to not demonstrate clarity in ministry, but unfortunately, many still do. It will take a great deal of work for this type of clarity to evolve, but when it does, there will be no turning back. This clarity will quickly become the ongoing expectation, and every volunteer who is serious about children's ministry will be thrilled that everyone is serving in unison.

The research results revealed that at least one volunteer observed the need for clearly defined roles and responsibilities. In

---

26. Finzel, *Top Ten Mistakes*, Location 2225–41.
27. Stanley et al., *7 Practices*, 65–66.

another question in which volunteers were asked about whether victories were celebrated, some 41 percent did not select a "Yes" or "No" answer, but commented in the "other" box in which written comments could be made. Some of the comments made regarding celebrating victories included "we celebrate our volunteers by choosing a volunteer of the month and they are recognized and given a small gift," another volunteer commented, "We are a small congregation and all wins are shared with a joyful heart one to one." With the exception of the "myself" comment, the other two comments mentioned are not bad in and of themselves, but they do not communicate much in the way of substance.

None of the three comments mentioned here reveal much about what the children's ministry volunteers were trying to achieve. No one said, "We celebrate as a team when a child comes to Christ" or "We celebrate when a family member or family unit has come to Christ or made a renewed commitment to follow after Christ." Perhaps the reason is that volunteers were unable to provide clear answers to this survey question was that they do not know what constitutes a "Win."

The term, "Win," would be defined as anything the children's ministry leadership has projected to volunteers that has been defined as a success. In other words, how do the children's ministry volunteers know when they are winning? Would it be the number of diapers changed in the nursery? Or perhaps it concerns how many children are in attendance. Does it focus on how many children were invited by the volunteer or how many children's ministry volunteers simply showed up? Does it center on which volunteer cleans up after the ministry time is completed, which volunteer transports children to church, or which volunteer likes recruiting other volunteers?

These are all tasks that a children's ministry might complete at any given ministry appointment within the church, but do they reveal that the volunteer is winning? The volunteer may think that these are what help them "Win" in the role they are serving in at church, but do they? Once again, how can they know if they are winning? A "Win" is something that children's ministry leadership needs to define for their volunteers. If there is an issue with clarity in the children's ministry, the volunteer could think that doing the above ministry tasks constitutes winning in their personal ministry.

Ministries that will do the hard work of clarifying the win will energize their volunteers and the ministry will greatly benefit from this practice. Unfortunately, many ministries fail to take the time to demonstrate this clarity within their ministries.

> Most organizations have written clever mission statements and carefully craft their values. But few organizations have summed up in a simple phrase what a win looks like at every level of the organization. You can't stop at the top of the organization. The principle will only help you become more effective if the practice is carried through to the levels where practical ministry is happening.[28]

These words ring true in that it seems almost every church has a catchy vision statement or phrase that captures the essence of who the church is. The problem is (as Stanley alludes to here) that the vision statement rarely moves through the levels of the organization, and children's ministry is sometimes one of the last ministries in which a win is defined. If this is the case, it is simply unacceptable, as the church, more than any organization on the planet, has no time to waste.

Every child that enters the doors of the ministry represents an opportunity to influence generations that follow with the gospel of Jesus Christ. The church must seize the moment to clarify what the successful path is for its ministries and volunteers because this is an urgent matter. There is additional danger if children's ministry leadership does not do the work of clarifying the "Win."

As anyone in ministry leadership knows, morale is important and this can be a morale killer. Stanley states,

> Nothing hinders morale more than when team members with separate agendas are pulling against one another.

---

28. Stanley et al., *7 Practices*, 83.

THE DISCUSSION

When this happens, it is usually because those in charge have not taken the time to clarify the win for the team. As long as the "win" is unclear, you force your team to define what a win looks like.[29]

The sad part of this scenario is that it is usually not the fault of the volunteers when they begin to pursue their own agendas while serving. They do this because they want to succeed, and they begin to do what they know to do in order to win. If this type of chaos continues, the ministry is negatively impacted and volunteers suddenly cease to show up to serve. It is not fair to the children's ministry volunteer to have to clarify the win for their ministry, but they will if no one else does, and the ministry results of this can be disastrous. The debriefings that were mentioned earlier may not be deemed productive for leaders who have not clarified the "Win."

To sum up, it is important to note that children's ministry volunteers love clarity. Why would anyone not want to see a clear picture of a ministry they are serving in or considering serving in, especially when it concerns ministry to children? Volunteers want to know how to win, they want to thrive in their role, they want to see children come to Christ, they want to see families grow closer to God as a result of the churches ministry to children and families, and they want to honor God in their service. The commitment level involved in any children's ministry is such that a volunteer would be lacking in common sense to take on this volunteer role without desiring to excel in it.

As such, the next section will outline the need for training of the children's ministry volunteer after clarity of purpose and mission has been achieved. These important components of children's ministry must coexist in order for effective volunteer development to take place. The children's ministry volunteer wants to win. They need to know how this is done in their church, which is where training comes into the picture.

---

29. Stanley et al., *7 Practices*, 72.

Children's Ministry Volunteers' Need for Training

The number one response to the question, "Name 1 thing that you believe would enhance the health and overall impact of your church's children's ministry volunteer experience," from volunteers in the research was "training." Volunteers have to be equipped for the work of the ministry or a disservice has been committed to the body of Christ, including the children who are in the care and ministry of the volunteer. The goal of this section is not to provide an exhaustive plan to train children's ministry volunteers, because every church is different. Each church has its own identity, and unless it is copying the vision of another church, it should have its own mission, core values, and expectations for anyone who wishes to serve in children's ministry. It is simply not profitable for anyone serving in children's ministry to be asked to do something without the proper training and knowledge needed to accomplish the ministry.

No one in a proper mental state would ever hand the keys to their car to a child and ask them to go to the store and buy groceries for them. This is (basically) what is happening when a church hands off a group of children in a nursery setting to someone who has no training for that specific ministry. No one would do that with their child (or vehicle), but those serving with children for some time have probably observed a similar obtuseness at some point. A church is asking for trouble when this is allowed, and one only needs to read the newspaper to occasionally see some of the issues that are flowing from the church, in part due to lack of training and ministry oversight.

Lack of volunteer training displays a lack of care for the volunteer and the ministry. Churches that truly value their volunteers through training that truly nurtures the volunteer will almost always add more volunteers.[30] Perhaps if more churches would truly invest in the volunteers they already have, they would not need to fret and worry about the number of volunteers they have. Training

---

30. Anderson and Fox, *Volunteer Church*, 33.

THE DISCUSSION

alone has the potential to revolutionize a stagnant volunteer ministry and is something every volunteer needs anyway.

According to Mavity, "Training is providing input, in various forms, to influence a person's future actions, attitudes, and behaviors. You'll need to train your volunteers so that they achieve the specific ministry outcomes you desire."[31] Once again, the win needs to be defined in terms of mission and core values, and even the behaviors that need to be exhibited by the volunteer should be part of the training that takes place.

An important concept in the training of children's ministry volunteers (and one that may assist with alleviating future frustration and disappointment) is that training actually begins the moment a children's ministry leader or children's ministry pastor begins the recruiting process. At this point, the ministry leader needs to be able to answer most of the questions a potential volunteer might have and should be able to immediately point them to the next steps that are required to begin serving in children's ministry. The potential volunteer should walk away knowing at least some of the important aspects of the ministry after a few conversations with a children's ministry leader or pastor. In a smaller church, this may always be the entry-level training for the prospective volunteer, but larger churches may provide an ongoing orientation, which is sort of a disguised recruiting tool that transitions into a training tool.

The orientation lays out the process required for potential children's ministry volunteers, which may lead to an opportunity for the volunteer to actually observe ministry firsthand and to prayerfully assess whether children's ministry is where God wants them to serve. This observation period will probably not be a detailed training, but could be considered the first steps toward gaining insights into how the ministry operates and who key members of the leadership team are. 12Stone Church in the Atlanta area offers a model as described above and is illustrated below.[32]

---

31. Mavity, *Your Volunteers*, Location 669.
32 12Stone Church, "Children's Ministry Volunteer Training."

71

> **BECOMING A PART OF THE TEAM!**
>
> To provide the safest possible environment for our kids and the most rewarding experience for our leaders all volunteers must complete the following process:
>
> **ORIENTATION**
> Attend a Children's Ministry New Volunteer Orientation.
>
> **APPLICATION**
> Complete a Children's Ministry Application, including a background check.
>
> **CONVERSATION**
> An interview with a Children's Ministry Leader.
>
> **OBSERVATION**
> Observe ministry area with an established volunteer for 2-6 weeks for training and assimilation.
>
> **INVITATION**
> Receive an invitation to the join team along with an official volunteer t-shirt!

Figure 4: 12Stone Church Team Process

At 12Stone Church, it would be very difficult for a potential volunteer to not get off to a good start in their ministry to children. The church has an excellent model for helping potential volunteers not only make an informed decision about becoming a children's ministry volunteer, but also to observe different children's ministry venues (for up to six weeks) as they prayerfully make their decision. This system is so much better than someone being thrown into an area of children's ministry just because they hinted to someone that they might be interested. If a potential volunteer does choose to begin serving on a regular basis, they will, of course, need to engage in other training provided by the

THE DISCUSSION

children's ministry team, but again, this simple process is setting the potential volunteer up for success.

It is worth noting that successful children's ministry training is not just for the church to provide. The potential or existing volunteer should have a hunger to learn and grow as a ministry volunteer in this area. This point reverts back to the comments made on recruiting. As Heusser states, "We must take seriously the selection process and each potential volunteer should be considered in light of the job needs and his or her interests, skills and abilities."[33] The church has the responsibility to train and equip, but the best volunteers are willing to go out themselves and seek tools that will sharpen the great work with children and families that they provide.

The initial conversations that occur in recruitment should put the onus upon the volunteer that although the church will encourage them and provide training opportunities, the volunteer needs to understand that their overall growth in the ministry is up to them. If a volunteer signals in the initial training that they have no desire or interest to be equipped, it should be a sign that being a volunteer in children's ministry may not be a good fit for both parties. Training is not something that is optional and should not be viewed this way by both the church and the volunteer. The following are four ways that a volunteer can take training upon themselves for growth and development as a children's ministry volunteer:

1. Attend a conference. Hopefully, this would be church sponsored and the church would assist with the cost, but even if it does not, attending a conference once a year will sharpen one and serve as a reminder as to how important children's ministry is. Every children's ministry volunteer should attend a conference or workshop every year.

2. Network with other children's ministry volunteers and leaders. Networking can also be a great way to be sharpened as well to gain new ideas from other volunteers in churches across the country or the region in which a volunteer serves.

---

33. Heusser, *Helping Church Workers Succeed*, 43.

3. Read—readers are leaders, and reading is vital for ministry volunteers. Volunteers who are serious about developing will take it upon themselves to read books and journals that will encourage and sharpen them. Every church should have a library or be moving towards having a library where this type of resource is accessible to volunteers. If not accessible through the church, a volunteer should subscribe to materials mentioned above if at all possible.

4. Take an online class through a Christian college. More and more universities are offering classes on a plethora of topics at no cost to individuals, although typically, there is no academic credit that can be earned for the class offering. This could be a great opportunity to learn more about issues facing children's ministries (if taken through a Christian university), but taking a course on child development through a secular university could provide some unique insights and helps into the development of children and the special needs that they each have.[34]

The aforementioned suggestions are some things volunteers can do on their own to provide training to themselves, but, of course, the church has a role to play in this as well. With so many ways to provide training, the church has to take on the responsibility to make this happen. There are many ways that training can be provided, which is fantastic because all volunteers learn differently. There needs to be varied content and varied length with the offered training, and special events throughout the year should be considered before offering training.

For example, it would probably not be a good idea to hold a lengthy training on meeting the emotional needs of a child the week before Christmas, as attendance is likely to be low. Greg Baird provided some great insights for churches to keep in mind as they prepare for and then execute training with volunteers. Baird said,

> No one wants to fail, and if they are giving their time and effort to ministry, they do want to do it right – and

---

34. Ervin, *Best Practices*, 168–71.

they need to be trained in order for that to happen. If this is true, then make your training: easy to access (offer it through multiple avenues); to the point—no single training should take long to complete; immediately applicable (go light on theory and heavy on practical application); engaging—enjoyable to participate in; beneficial—feed them, give them gifts and offer practical tools to use this week in their ministry.[35]

Using email and brief training videos are great ways to provide important information and reminders to volunteers, but there is also nothing like personal training from someone who is serving in children's ministry, perhaps held every other month on topics related to children's ministry and volunteers.

As a matter of fact, using the excuse that volunteers are busy and moving completely to video training or emails may not prove to be beneficial. Children's ministry volunteers—and other volunteers for this matter—need to occasionally hear directly from their respective leaders, and face-to-face instruction allows this to happen. Training is also a great way to continue to clarify the win and the vision as volunteers are trained to reach children for Christ and carry out the vision of their local church.

Final Thoughts

In this chapter, we have issued a challenge to all readers through the four essential volunteer developmental stories. Presumably, there will be someone who reads this and says, "Oh yes, my church needs this." Our desire is that through the research findings and discussion of the project, pastors and children's ministry leaders will either renew or initiate efforts to provide a system in which volunteers can thrive. Moreover, we hope that greater support in the form of coaching volunteers onto greater levels of excellence and ministry productivity might be provided for each children's ministry volunteer.

35. Baird, "7 Things We Need to Understand."

Additionally, the hope is that greater clarity might be provided if this is lacking, so that children's volunteers understand the reasons for their ministry to children (along with the role they play in their service to children). Finally, we hope that there might be an increased willingness to train children's ministry volunteers for kingdom-building, with church leaders begging to comprehend the value that children's ministry volunteers feel when they are trained with excellence.

5

The Solution

It is always helpful to see an example of something done well. The following case studies are not perfect examples of churches that are excelling in the development of their children's ministry volunteers, but they do exemplify strategies that we believe will strengthen your children's ministry volunteer program. In this chapter, examples are provided from Crossings Community Church of Oklahoma City, Oklahoma; North Point Church of Alpharetta, Georgia; 12Stone Church of Lawrenceville, Georgia; and Saddleback Church of Lake Forest, California.

We would encourage readers to take the opportunity to personally visit some of the churches mentioned in this chapter if the opportunity ever arose. Certainly, there is no doubt that many churches are developing very healthy volunteer teams that are effectively reaching children. They may not receive great notice, but their contributions to their volunteers are significant and will be rewarded by the Lord. Through research, we felt these churches were excelling in one or more of the four components that children's ministry volunteers were literally begging for at church. We pray that the provided case studies will serve as a catalyst to sharpen your children's ministry volunteer ministry.

Children's Ministry Volunteer System Example

One church that provides a good example of having a quality volunteer system for children's ministry would be that of Crossings Community Church, which is located in the Oklahoma City area.

Crossings Community is a multi-site ministry that reaches thousands in this area of the midwestern United States. This church was chosen because of the incredible technology that it has in place for volunteers to begin service, as well as the language that the church uses when recruiting children's ministry volunteers. If someone is interested in serving with children at Crossings Community, he or she can go to the church website and express interest by completing an online contact form. After the form is completed, a representative from the ministry contacts the potential volunteer to follow up.

One of the unique things about the system at Crossing Community is that the website has a running number of volunteer opportunities available. At the time of this writing, there were over three hundred volunteer opportunities available for volunteers to engage in, with many opportunities available for children's ministry volunteers. Approximately 30 to 45 percent of the volunteer opportunities listed are related to children's ministry. This number fluctuates while viewing the website and, of course, goes down when positions are filled and up as the ministry sees more needs at any of their campuses.

Additionally, attached to the volunteer interest form is a volunteer placement quiz, which the church uses to assess the spiritual gifts of potential volunteers. So, before the ministry representatives ever meet with potential volunteers, they are aware of their ministry interests and already have knowledge of how God has wired the potential volunteer for ministry. Additionally, there is a brief job description available for most of the volunteer opportunity links, almost all of which are on the website.

Another area of the system that is well done is that the volunteer page provides a section dedicated to volunteer stories. This section has short articles, which appear to be written by the volunteer themselves, describing their service in children's ministry (and other ministries of the church). They usually speak to the fact that the ministry has been a blessing to them because of the opportunity they have had to serve. This is a great opportunity to share "Wins" for the entire church to see, and for that matter, the entire world to see.

THE SOLUTION

This system allows for children's ministry volunteers to have a sense that they are succeeding by making news on the church website, and it is a fabulous recruiting tool as well, since potential volunteers can see clearly that children's ministry is valued highly by the church and volunteers are experiencing life change as a result of being involved in children's ministry. One final note (that displays a nice touch to the volunteer entry system that Crossings Community Church has in place) is that the church has paid staff that works exclusively with volunteer development and assimilation. There is a paid director listed along with her assistant.

The staff members' email addresses are provided along with a phone number for the volunteer ministry. Although it is difficult to tell exactly what happens with volunteers once they get connected, it is easy to see on the front end that this is a church dedicated to volunteer development and that they value the ministry that volunteers bring to Crossings Community Church.

Other churches that bring value to the concept of having a system in place and are worthy of further research are Wooddale Church in Eden Prairie, Minnesota, and the Journey Church in New York City. Both of the pastors of these churches have written extensively on their experience with volunteering systems, too.

From what we have observed, both churches have benefited from systems that have produced strong volunteer ministries. Additionally, for those who serve in a smaller community with limited resources, this is an great example that one could use to cast vision for developing a volunteer ministry system that better meets their needs.

Children's Ministry Volunteer Clarity Example

North Point Community Church in Alpharetta, Georgia, ministers to thousands of children in the Atlanta area and, through satellite churches, throughout the country. The church is in the top five in attendance in the nation and is known for its ministry throughout the world. According to the church's website, "Currently, North Point Ministries has over 23,000 adults participating in worship at six churches each Sunday. In addition, over 14,000 children and students meet in small groups while their parents attend worship."[1]

We visited North Point ministries for conferences (and a few other related events on several occasions) and have witnessed firsthand how clarity plays a role in the impressive functioning of all volunteer ministries. A tour of the children's ministry facility is enough to leave anyone in awe of the quality ministry that the church has with children. Children and children's ministry volunteers matter at North Point, and this comes across loud and clear to visitors and attendees of the church. One can quickly perceive that the church is well-organized, for both ministry and volunteers are on the same page. The "Win" has been clarified and for the most part, and everyone knows the "Why" as it relates to ministry service.

We spoke with several volunteers from varying parts of the North Point ministry on a recent visit. Without hesitation, volunteers were all aware of why they were doing what they were doing, and they could all communicate the vision for the church, and attach the purpose of their ministry to the vision of the church. This was not always the case at North Point, however, as Andy Stanley describes in his book, *7 Practices of Effective Ministry*.

It was actually through children's ministries that North Point's leadership began to understand the importance of clarifying the win with children's ministry volunteers. Issues began to arise early on in the children's ministries of the church as some volunteers did not feel they were developing quality relationships with kids attending the UpStreet children's ministry program. This led the church to recast a vision for this particular ministry. In other words, the "win" had not been clarified enough, and some disconnect began to appear in the ministry. According to Stanley, this lack of clarity caused the church to begin to clarify roles and recast the vision for this area of children's ministry.[2]

Currently, the purpose of UpStreet is stated in the following:

1. North Point Community Church, "History."
2. Stanley et al., *7 Practices*, 74.

UpStreet is our small group environment for elementary-aged kids. But here's what we really believe is important for you to know about UpStreet: when our kids show up on Sunday morning, we believe that the Bible should NEVER be boring, that worship can be really loud, and that the best leaders ALWAYS care. In other words, we want to make sure that our kids experience the acceptance and joy of knowing their Heavenly Father. That's what UpStreet is all about! We want our kids to know: I need to make the wise choice. I can trust God no matter what. I should treat others the way I want to be treated. Everything that we teach flows from these Three Basic Truths. The purpose of UpStreet is to connect our kindergarteners through 5th graders into a small group where they will begin to unpack what it means to have a growing relationship with Jesus Christ. We want our kids to see how God's word applies to their lives and how his truth really tells them how to live. Every week we connect our kids to the same small group leaders, giving them another trusted relationship that will help connect them to a relationship with their Heavenly Father."[3]

So, for children's ministry volunteers at North Point, the "Win" that has been clarified for them is that their main goal is to serve and equip children to make wise choices in all that they do. The second goal is to communicate and live their lives in a way that shows children that they can trust God and that He is worthy of their trust—the children can count on God to come through for them. The last thing is that children's ministry volunteers are to model what treating others God's way is all about. Children may not leave the children's ministry with a comprehensive understanding of all stories from the Bible, but they will leave knowing more about the three biblical purposes that make up the UpStreet children's ministry. If curriculum needs to be written, the topics are already in front of the writers because the direction for the ministry is clear.

The purpose and value of the children's ministry have been clarified to children, parents, and to the volunteers. Everyone

3. North Point Ministries, "Children's Environments."

knows what the goal is, and perhaps more importantly, everyone knows what the goal of UpStreet is not. When it is time for training, these purposes fuel how the "Why" behind any training that takes place with children's ministry volunteers. Everything will be geared toward helping children enter the sixth grade with the knowledge stemming from those three purposes. If this happens, then everyone celebrates that as a "Win" at North Point. Volunteers at North Point would say that the mission had been accomplished.

Children's Ministry Volunteer Coaching Example

The final two examples in the all-important arena of developing children's ministry volunteers are found within the ministry of 12Stone Church in Lawrenceville, Georgia. The children's pastor at 12Stone Church, Lynn, ministers to thousands of children on a weekly basis in numerous locations around the Atlanta area. 12Stone is an excellent example of functional volunteer ministry training and coaching as well. Other churches do a wonderful job with training, but few churches have a coaching system in place for children's ministry volunteers. 12Stone was the only church that we could find which had implemented coaching into its ongoing volunteer development. This reveals that many churches are lagging behind in this important aspect of development.

Of the coaching structure that the children's ministry has in place, children's pastor Lynn states,

> We have a position called volunteer coach, and this person has 10 people in their small group. They lead weekly huddles, reach out to their volunteers outside of church, encourage them, influence them, pray for them and pour into them, plan fun events for them outside of church to build community. I meet with my coaches monthly (as a group and individually) and pour into them as they lead their small group."[4]

4. Howard, "Keeping Your Children's Ministry Volunteers."

THE SOLUTION

There may not be a need for a coach in this area for smaller churches until attendance reaches the 150 to 200 range in attendance, but the sooner this can be implemented into the life of the children's ministry, the better. One way that a coach could multiply their impact is the idea of the coach serving as a small group leader of the children's ministry volunteers. This may be better than having a traditional ministry coach, who most likely coaches on a one-on-one basis. This approach provides the coach with an even better opportunity to get to know the volunteers and address the spiritual and ministry needs that children's ministry volunteers may have. There is no question that, between the needs of the children being ministered to and that the personal needs of the volunteer, there will always be things to discuss.

The children's ministry volunteer coach is highlighted in the "12Stone Volunteer Handbook." The role of the children's ministry volunteer is defined here, but is also listed as a volunteer opportunity, which allows a potential volunteer to go through the process of possibly serving in this role at 12Stone.

> ## The Children's Ministry Team
>
> ### WHO'S ON THE TEAM?
>
> **CHILDREN'S MINISTRY TEAM LEADER** (or Children's Pastor): A staff or volunteer coordinator or director who is responsible for all aspects of Children's Ministry at a specific campus
>
> ### MINISTRY LEADER/COORDINATOR:
> A staff or volunteer coordinator who is responsible for all aspects of a specific ministry area across all services
>
> ### SERVICE LEADER:
> A staff or volunteer leader who is responsible for all aspects of a ministry area during one service
>
> ### COACH:
> A volunteer who leads and cares for other volunteers within a specific service and ministry area
>
> ### VOLUNTEER:
> A Children's Ministry volunteer who is at least 16 years of age and serves in any area of Children's Ministry. A 16 or 17 year old may only serve as a 3rd or subsequent leader for children less than 3 years of age.
>
> ### STUDENT VOLUNTEER:
> A Children's Ministry volunteer who has completed 5th grade and is less than 16 years of age may:
> Serve with children no younger than crawlers
> Play with children on the floor,
> but may not pick up or hold children
> Only serve as 3rd or subsequent volunteer in a room.

Figure 5: 12Stone Church Volunteer Handbook

THE SOLUTION

Children's Ministry Volunteer Training Example

Saddleback Community Church in Lake Forest, California, is often known as the church that Rick Warren pastors, but the church also has a vibrant children's ministry that reaches thousands of children in southern California. The children's pastor at the church, Steve, has spent years developing the children's ministry at Saddleback. As with any successful children's ministry, Steve describes the all-important area of training of volunteers as being essential to the success that they have had in children's ministry. Affirming this, Don Cousins once wrote, "If you hold a leadership position but are not equipping the saints for the work of service, then you are not a leader. You may hold the position; you may have the title; you may be called a leader; but you're not a leader as the Bible defines it, because leadership means equipping."[5] Training and equipping go hand-in-hand, and without them, there can be no development.

Their church pastor, Steve believes that churches need to be strategic and intentional about training volunteers. In some ways, this goes back to what was previously mentioned about having a system of ministry. Ongoing training needs to be a built-in part of the system of every church in order to effectively equip volunteers for service.

At Saddleback, much of the focus on children's volunteer training centers on the development of the volunteers' gifts and their skills. The children's pastor is quick to point out that there is no one-size-fits-all approach to training children's ministry volunteers.[6] The training at Saddleback is not so much about having meetings and watching videos; it is more about the culture that has been built in Saddleback's children's ministries. Meetings and other tools are used, but the main focus is slowly exposing volunteers to the culture that has been established and in a way that allows volunteers to be carefully trained for ministry with children.

As an example of how Saddleback trains children's ministry volunteers, their children's pastor states,

---

5. Cousins, *Experiencing Leadership*, 35.
6. Adams, *Children's Ministry on Purpose*, 175.

For each ministry season, our children's ministry follows a theme. We use ministry themes for two primary reasons: to create alignment and bring focus to our team. I determine the theme and develop that theme to teach, train, and encourage our team members throughout the year. The theme is designed to equip paid and volunteer team members. This equipping plan and process involves weekly connections in our Pre-Game meeting thirty minutes before the start of each service, monthly training, age (or grade) level training, quarterly training, and our annual gathering to kick off the new ministry season.[7]

The training is nothing drastic and seems to be more or less on a quarterly basis. so the time constraints of volunteers' needs are met. Yet, the vision is cast and volunteers are trained for an approximate three months of ministry before the next theme emerges. At Saddleback, once volunteers are recruited and trained, they are then empowered for ministry and released to serve. In between these trainings, Saddleback children's ministries use varying forms of communication to continue to clarify and drive the ministry strategy.

Saddleback also empowers volunteers by providing other ministry roles and responsibilities as God blesses the volunteers' gifts and abilities. Like North Point and 12Stone, Saddleback employs a coaching system about which children's pastor Steve raves at the positive effect on their children's workers. Intertwined coaching and training go a long way toward creating a healthy children's ministry volunteer team that will make a great impact in the lives of children for the kingdom of God.

Suggestions for Further Research

We were advised that this project would be challenging due in part because of the limited research available on children's ministry volunteers. This individual was correct in this assessment. There are

---

7. Adams, *Children's Ministry on Purpose*, 188–89.

only a few books that portray the plans and strategies of existing churches children's ministry volunteer development, and there are almost no peer-reviewed research articles on this topic.

Some suggestions for further research would include more church-based studies on children's ministry volunteers to include their perceptions of children's ministry, their thoughts on improving it, and how they view the effectiveness of it, to name a few. Something also beneficial would be studies on children's ministry volunteer training, the role of senior pastor and children's volunteers, and how effective children's ministry volunteers are in the church today. There is minimal measurement of the aforementioned options, so there are difficulties in assessing the accuracy of the state of children's ministry and the volunteers who serve in children's ministry.

Also, the application of the principles in this chapter was taken primarily from megachurches. These churches were the only churches that we discovered which had documented their use of these ministry principles. There is a great need for research in smaller churches that may be utilizing some of the principles outlined in this project in megachurches. Hopefully, this work will help other researchers expound more on this topic so that the church can be built up through greater volunteer service in children's ministries across the world.

6

Epilogue

This topic was challenging to write on because I have never served in children's ministry on a permanent basis—mostly because it never seemed to be my personal calling, gifting, or passion to do so. I have always been heavily involved in other areas of the ministry as either a staff member or in a layperson's role. There have been occasional times that I have stepped in to serve in A.W.A.N.A. when needed or as a nursery substitute with my wife when volunteer attendance was low on a given Sunday. This was usually the result of poor planning by the ministry coordinator, bad communication, or to fill in for an absentee volunteer (expected or unexpected).

My decision to engage in service during the above times stems from my belief that Christians need to be ready and willing to roll up their sleeves to meet the need right in front of us. This type of scenario is the primary way in which I have been involved in serving children. Although I have been in staff roles with general oversight of certain areas of children's ministry at different times, I never truly understood the importance of children's ministry volunteers until my wife embraced this role and served the Lord with her gifts in it. There is no doubt that this project could have been completed much sooner (and with greater ease) had I chosen a different topic.

Writing on church growth or small groups would have been a breeze in light of the challenges associated with this topic. However, after observing my wife serve and assisting her when possible, I began to gain a greater appreciation for the dedicated children's ministry volunteers who served weekly with smiles on their face (most

EPILOGUE

of the time anyway), and who (for the most part) simply wanted to see children ministered to in a fun and welcoming environment. The more that I observed and the more that I listened to my wife speak of her ministry experience, in just about every church that I visited, the more cognizant I became that much improvement was needed in this area of ministry.

Out of the several churches where I was either on staff or serving as a layperson, I can only recall one of those churches putting forth their absolute best effort in regard to children's ministry volunteers and the children's ministry as a whole. At the time of this writing, that one church has begun to lose focus on this ministry and its volunteers. During the timeframe that this church excelled with children's ministry, its ministry to children was not just occasionally mentioned; it was a priority in all that the church did. When it came time for vacation Bible school (VBS), there were some eighty volunteers who took time off work just to have the opportunity to serve children.

It was because of these experiences that I felt burdened to research and write in order to help churches renew their efforts to make children's ministry and children's ministry volunteers a greater priority. I was unable to shake the feeling that I had inside whenever I thought about most of the children's ministries that I have observed within the ministries in which my wife and I have participated. I am saddened by the poor quality, lack of vision, and lack of focus in this area of church ministry that I have observed.

Although several of the ministries that we were a part of touted their allegiance to children and children's ministry volunteers, we rarely saw this on a weekly basis. Most of the churches infrequently (if ever) provided any substantive training for volunteers. In almost all the churches, the vision for children's ministry lacked substance and clarity. We remember very little training (outside of vacation Bible school training) that our churches offered every year. If we were to ask ten different children's ministry volunteers how the vision of the church related to children's ministry, we would most likely garner a different answer from each of the volunteers.

We also rarely heard anything in the church service about children's ministry or what was taking place with children. I understand the primary purpose of the pulpit (and the role of the pastor is mainly preaching), but an occasional word about this vital ministry goes a long way in building ministry momentum. It reminds volunteers that their service is vital to the development of children (and to ongoing ministry efforts in the church). This also communicates that the pastor cares about what is occurring and is invested in all that is taking place with children and those ministering to the children. When this never occurs, the lack of communication still sends a message—that this particular ministry of the church is a trivial concern. It is just something the church offers parents so that they can come to the service.

Many times, when we did hear a pastor speak about the children's ministry, it was in the form of an emergency plea for volunteers because the nursery or other parts of the children's ministry were inadequately staffed for ministry. We observed that this type of plea worked for the short term, and there would be at least a small influx of those wishing to serve in children's ministry, but it rarely helped in addressing long-term needs. The volunteers who stepped up after a plea were usually moving into what would only be an interim role for them, although this was never stated by the volunteer on the front end of their commitment.

My wife and I have been serving in church ministry in some capacity as a couple for over twenty-one years. During this time, we have never once heard a clear vision for children's ministry from a senior pastor during a request for additional volunteers. Even moreso, we have never heard a clear reason as to how children's ministry fits into the overall vision of the church. This has typically just been a cry for help, almost as if one were in a ship in the middle of the ocean and a large hole suddenly appears in the hull of the ship.

In other words, we have never heard from pastors the "Why" of children's ministry or how potential children's ministry volunteers can fulfill the vision of the church to reach children. We have never seen the vision attached to the need in any of the churches to which we have belonged. We have been a part of churches ranging in size from four hundred members to ten thousand in attendance, and not once have we observed the aforementioned taking place. I long for the day that I see this occurring on a regular basis because the church has so much to gain when this happens.

Personal Failures in Developing Children's Ministry Volunteers

If the previous rhetoric sounds overly harsh, this is not the intent (although pastoral leadership plays an incredible role in the effectiveness of children's ministry). In reflecting on our own ministry from a pastoral perspective, we would say that we failed to incorporate some of the very things that have been mentioned in this project and, as a result, failed some very good children's ministry volunteers along the way. As young leaders, we did not have a clear grasp of some of the things that were mentioned in chapter 4 because of lack of training—coupled with the fact that children's ministry was not our primary responsibility in the church.

We might have been responsible for some oversight of children's ministry, but we were pulled in the direction of other ministries because that was what we were requested to do. If we could go back and do it all over again, we would be sure that children's ministry was viewed as a priority—even above other ministries of the church. We would be sure the "Win" for volunteers was clarified, that training was done consistently and with excellence, that a coaching model of support was put into place for children's ministry volunteers, and that there was a system developed to ensure children's ministry volunteers knew their role and the part they played in the ministry.

Despite the poor leadership that we had in place over children's ministry, God blessed the ministry, and it grew. However, with coaching, clarity, systems, and training, it is painful to imagine all that could have been accomplished in the development of volunteers and the kingdom in the community. We now know better and hope others will learn from our mistakes.

A Challenge to Pastors

We bring up the aforementioned because we know the challenges that pastors face in operating a ministry on a day-to-day basis. Volunteer development is difficult on any level, but if in a small-to-medium sized church, children's ministry and children's ministry volunteer development can be extremely challenging. These challenges are real, and most ministers authentically have a heart for children. Most pastors want to see a vibrant children's ministry taking place in their church—one in which glorifies God and builds up the kingdom.

This will not happen on its own; pastors have to be the voice for children's ministry and its volunteers from the pulpit. The senior pastor's passion for children's ministry and its volunteers will go a long way towards developing the volunteers and the ministry. If the pastor is not passionate about children's ministry (misunderstanding its importance), then the ministry needs to be delegated to someone who is. This person needs visibility and the opportunity to use his or her voice to represent children and the volunteers.

In addition, we would beg the children's ministry point person for the church to clarify the "Win" for the volunteers. Volunteers need to know from their leader what success looks like for their ministry. The vision and goals for this ministry should be crystal clear. The pastor must ensure that there is a system in place for volunteer training and the overall development of the children's ministry. Failure to do this could, in time, be detrimental to the impact that children's ministry will have on the church and community. The bottom line is that churches that are winning with their children's ministry volunteers have a system in place. They use the system, and the system usually produces results or notifies leadership when there are issues that need to be resolved.

Coaching children's ministry volunteers may be a new concept to many reading this book. Why not give this a try in your church? If not now, this could be something that you cast a vision for in the future. It is difficult to provide ongoing care, support, and ministry renewal apart from a coaching ministry. We have never met a person in ministry who was under the direction of a coach who did not grow and develop into a better minister, and we have never met anyone who regretted having a coach to work with them and support them. Coaching truly helps volunteers go further and faster. This is a positive situation for everyone involved if it is well planned and executed. With the enormous responsibility that children's ministry volunteers have, it is incumbent upon the church to support them. Although coaching is recommended, if coaching is not possible, it will be necessary to find something that will assist volunteers in this way.

Lastly, children's ministry volunteers need to be trained. The pastor cannot do everything nor is not expected to, but volunteers need to know how to fulfill their ministry in a way that is rewarding for children and fulfilling for the volunteer. Volunteers want to see life change happen as much as anyone; they just do not always know how to carry out their ministry. Training them for the task of ministry is one of the greatest things that any church does, and volunteers appreciate seeing the results of the use of new insights into children and families as well as new methods of ministry to children.

Volunteers desire to be challenged to go beyond the mundane and reach children for Christ. Will you be the pastor that takes training to the next level at your church, using varying methods of delivery with stories of life change and celebration of wins along the way? Your children's ministry volunteers want this. Will you provide this for them?

A Challenge to Volunteers

For those reading our book who serve as children's ministry volunteers, we want to say, "Thank you." Your service is making a difference in the lives of children in your church, and as those children develop into passionate followers of Christ, your influence extends to the community and beyond. We know this ministry may seem overlooked by other ministries that get more of the spotlight, but your ministry is so often life-changing for children. They may not exactly tell you what those changes are, but your words and demeanor, your teaching, and your stories of God working through your life are having a great impact.

Like many others with fond memories, I still remember Mrs. Bessie Hundley (now in heaven), a children's ministry volunteer from my home church who made a difference in my life. Her passion and energy for the Lord made a lasting impression on me. Her ministry was during the "flannelgraph" days of children's ministry, and I can still remember the stories that she would tell about biblical characters—along with the love and care she showed to each and every child.

Interestingly, one could say that Mrs. Hundley probably did not do very well in terms of clarifying the "Win" or training other volunteers. Back then, there was no thought of a ministry system, not to even mention of having a ministry coach. Despite this, that particular children's ministry thrived. Lives were changed, and today, there are many in full-time vocational ministry because of what was happening—because of her vibrant, intentional work.

So, why do pastors and churches need to embrace systems, coaching, clarity, and training today for children's ministry volunteers if they did not need it thirty years ago? This is a question worth contemplation, but, in short, culture has changed and the postmodern world is much more skeptical and subjective as it relates to how the church is viewed.

Unfortunately, due to the failures in the church, both morally and systemically, the church is not what it used to be in some ways. In the late 1970s, when we were young children, people went to church because this was something viewed as being noble to do. Church was the life of the community. There was more overall trust in the church, and people seemed to see it as a source of help that they were willing to lean upon without reservation. The new era of ministry brings with it more aloofness from church prospects, and many potential church attenders view the website of the church before they ever attend a service.

EPILOGUE

In part because of these reasons, systems, clarity, coaching, and training will play a role in the development of strong children's ministries and the volunteers who make this ministry happen every week. Our encouragement to you is to embrace these components of ministry, knowing that they are going to make you a better minister to children and, in turn, will make the overall ministry stronger.

We would also encourage you to work toward becoming a better children's ministry volunteer on your own. The primary person responsible for your development is you. The church has a responsibility to come alongside in this process, but development is ultimately your responsibility. Practically speaking, there are things leaders and servants need to participate in if God has truly called you to serve in this ministry. The following are eleven suggestions in light of the aforementioned:

1. Take time daily to pray for your church and the church leaders.
2. Take time daily to pray for the children who attend and for outreach opportunities in the community to reach more children.
3. Love the children that you serve each week. Do what you can to create a culture where children feel special and they know you care about them.
4. If there is a meeting for children's ministry volunteers, be in attendance and on time.
5. When serving children, wear a smile on your face and realize that you have one of the greatest opportunities on the planet. Children will know quickly whether or not you want to be around them. Make sure that the brief time you spend with them each week is quality time.
6. Be a team player as this shows the love and unity that children need to see in our actions. Children are watching and learning as adults interact with each other.

7. Commit fully to the Lord and to the children's ministries of your church.
8. Champion the children's ministry and be a voice of clarity concerning its purpose in the church. When you are asked about this ministry, know the answers. If you do not know them, begin to ask questions to ministry leaders.
9. Support the children's ministry system in place or pray for one to be implemented if needed.
10. Attend and participate in children's ministry training as much as possible.
11. Request a ministry coach to help develop your personal ministry or volunteer to coach other children's ministry volunteers as God opens this opportunity.

Closing Thoughts

One final thought for children's ministry volunteers is that what you are doing in the form of your service to the Lord is a good thing. 1 Thessalonians 3:13 encourages readers when it says, "As for you, brothers, do not grow weary in doing good."

Your service to the church is truly building the kingdom of God. For those who are nursery workers, it may not seem or smell this way when that dirty diaper is changed or the A.W.A.N.A. volunteer has to work with the dysfunctional behaviors of a second-grader who is disrupting the Bible memorization time, but you are doing good for the community of God.

Every time you answer the call to serve each week, you are doing good. Every time you diffuse an angry situation with a child, you are doing good. In every problem with children that you address, you are doing good. The church appreciates you, children love you, and as the Lord says, "You are doing good, keep on doing this great ministry to my children," because children matter!

Afterword

Recently, I asked the fifteen children surrounding me near the front of the stage to close their eyes as we paused and talked to God in prayer. I was attempting to transition from the short two-minute-long teaching about how prayer was simply talking to God like a friend. As I asked the children a simple question about how they talked to God, I received varied responses, spanning from a detailed description of discovering a recently lost family cat to forgiving a sibling that had been mean that week. These responses were accompanied by a gentle, entertained laughter from the adults who were listening.

So, I redirected the children and I began to pray through my wireless headset mic, "Dear God . . ." To my surprise, the little four-year-old boy sitting next to me, with his hands folded and his eyes closed earnestly looking upward, in a faint whisper audibly repeated, "Dear God." I paused, taken back by his sincerity and becoming immediately aware of the awesome gift and responsibility that unscripted moment occasioned. Although surrounded by adults gathered for communal worship, at that moment, the most important thing God was inviting me as a pastor to do was to guide this sweet boy in prayer. I did not instruct any of the children to repeat after me, but out of a spontaneous sincerity, this one young boy was looking to me to help him connect with God.

As I continued praying with the rhythmic pausing cadence, similar to marriage vows or a cross cultural translated sermon, I was increasingly aware of this sacred moment. I was helping this child to pray. I was giving him only a few words at a time to pray and—with all of his heart, soul, mind, and strength—he was loving and talking directly to God. His whisper was so faint that only one other person on the front row could even hear what he was saying or had any idea why my prayer cadence had so many mid-sentence-pauses throughout.

Perhaps my delivery and simplified prayer seemed odd to all the others who were only hearing my voice praying; yet, I knew the most important invitation by God in that moment was to contribute to this young child's spiritual formation—to help him grow in relationship with God through prayer. I had the weighty, awesome, and soul-shaping opportunity to help guide him to our living, active, divine father who is eager to connect with this young child. Although hidden to almost everyone else in the room, I am convinced that my simple act of guiding him in prayer was the most spiritually significant pastoral act that I participated in that Sunday gathering, which included proclaiming the Word of God and presiding over the sacrament of the Lord's Supper.

As a pastor for over twenty years, I often wonder if much of the brokenness within people's lives, which I have experienced in the messiness of pastoring in the local church, could be circumvented or possibly completely avoided if from a young age children were taught and molded what a growing relationship with God entails. Those who work with children are some of the most overlooked and misunderstood ministers within the whole church. Those brave enough to follow God's nudge into this loving and sacrificial service are more often than not, minimally trained and set loose with little direction or vision toward a greater end. Instead of being a potentially catapulting time of discipleship training for children, it can be reduced to simple childcare. Tragically, in people's most spiritually responsive years of childhood, Sunday school, and other forms of children's spiritual formation group are statistically not likely to help children along their steps of faith.

Warren and Knox contribute to this important conversation about children's spiritual formation within the local church. While emphasizing the primary role of parents training their children in the way they should go (Proverbs 22:6), the authors correctly represent the Christian community as an important incubator of

AFTERWORD

Christian faith formation for children. Historically tracing the communal role of influence that the greater Christian community has had upon children is a helpful contribution, which builds toward their final conclusions. The book has helped give greater historical and cultural awareness to the many dynamics that face the twenty-first century family, providing practical ways in which the Christian community can aid in the spiritual formation of children.

The authors have offered a thorough and thoughtful inquiry into the many faceted and complex issues effecting todays training of children within the local church. By emphasizing the holy and profound opportunity of contributing to the spiritual formation of children, Warren and Knox have encouraged a reassessment and reengagement with the importance of various ways the Christian community can proactively be involved with the spiritual formation of children.

Reverend Art Matheny, DMin
Pastor, T.R.U. Church
St. George, Kansas

Jennifer M. Matheny, PhD
Assistant Professor of Old Testament
Nazarene Theological Seminary
Kansas City, MO

Appendix A

Pastor and Children's Ministry Leader Interview Questions

Developing High Impact Childrens' Volunteers in the Local Church Survey

Pastoral Survey

1. A healthy volunteer experience is one in which the volunteer displays passion about their service in a way that spiritually impacts others while also bringing a sense of fulfillment to the volunteer. Do you believe your children's ministry volunteers are having a healthy experience serving in the children's ministries of your church?
2. Can children's ministry volunteers in your church clearly articulate the vision of the church?
3. Do you believe the vision of the church incorporates the value of children somewhere in its message?
4. Do you believe the children's ministry volunteer's service to the Lord in children's ministry is fulfilling the vision of the church?
5. Do you feel your church emphasizes the task more or the ministry more as it relates to volunteer service?
6. Do you believe current volunteer morale is high in the children's ministries of your church? If not why?

APPENDIX A: LEADER INTERVIEW QUESTIONS

7. Does your children's ministry leadership strive to discover if potential volunteers have been called to serve in children's ministry?

8. Do you believe your children's ministry volunteers walk with Christ is growing stronger because of their service to the Lord and His church in children's ministry?

9. Does your church invest heavily into the leadership development of children's ministry workers?

10. Does the church provide training to assist children's ministry volunteers with learning, developing, and then using their spiritual gifts?

11. If a children's ministry volunteer believed God was leading them to a different area of ministry within the church, do you feel there is freedom for them to explore this leading from God?

12. Does the children's ministry leadership in your church regularly show concern for the personal spiritual development of leaders through engagement, strategic planning and accountability?

13. Are victories celebrated in the children's ministry of your church? If yes, how so?

14. As a Pastor do you believe that you adequately support the children's ministry and children's ministry volunteers of your church?

15. Within the last year has the successful recruiting of children's ministry volunteer been more staff driven or volunteer driven (In other words who do you feel is most responsible for new children's ministry volunteers)?

16. Do you feel the current training for children's ministry in your church is contributing to the development of healthy, high impact children's volunteers?

APPENDIX A: LEADER INTERVIEW QUESTIONS

17. How much of a priority is church-wide prayer for the children's ministry and children's ministry volunteers in your church?

    a. Extremely important

    b. Important

    c. Somewhat important

    d. Not that important

18. Which phrase do you believe most individuals serving in children's ministry would believe the church views them as?

    a. "I am a ministry volunteer"

    b. "I am a ministry partner"

19. Name 1 thing that you believe would enhance the health and overall impact of your church's children's ministry volunteer experience?

20. What would you say is your greatest current frustration regarding children's ministry volunteers?

Appendix B

Children's Ministry Volunteer Interview Questions

Developing Healthy, High Impact Children's Volunteers in the Local Church Volunteer Survey

1. A healthy volunteer experience is one in which the volunteer displays passion about their service in a way that spiritually impacts others, while also bringing a sense of fulfillment to the volunteer. Are you currently having this type of experience as a volunteer in the children's ministry of your church?
2. Can you clearly articulate the vision of your church?
3. Do you believe the vision statement of the church incorporates the value of children somewhere in its message?
4. Do you believe your service to the Lord in children's ministry is fulfilling the vision of the church?
5. Within your ministry as a children's ministry volunteer do you feel the church emphasizes the task more or the ministry more as it relates to your service?
6. Do you believe current volunteer morale is high in the children's ministries of your church? If not why?
7. Do you believe God has called you to volunteer in children's ministry?
8. Do you believe your walk with Christ is growing stronger because of your service to the Lord as a children's ministry volunteer?

APPENDIX B: VOLUNTEER INTERVIEW QUESTIONS

9. Do you believe your church is invested in developing you as a children's ministry leader?
10. Do you know your spiritual gifts and are they being utilized within your children's ministry role?
11. If you believed God was leading you to a different area of ministry within the church, do you feel there is freedom to explore this leading from God?
12. Do you believe the children's ministry leadership actively shows concern for your personal spiritual development through engagement, strategic planning, and accountability?
13. Are victories celebrated amongst volunteer children's ministry staff? If yes, how so?
14. As a volunteer do you feel supported by your Lead/Sr. Pastor and other pastoral staff members? If yes, how so?
15. Within the last year have you personally been involved in the successful recruiting of another children's ministry volunteer?
16. Do you feel the current training for children's ministry in your church is contributing to the development of healthy, high impact children's volunteers?
17. When serving the Lord in children's ministry do you feel a strong sense that you are being prayed for or are being frequently lifted up in prayer by the church and church staff?
18. Which phrase best describes how you feel your ministry is viewed?
    a. "I am a ministry volunteer"
    b. "I am a ministry partner"
19. Name 1 thing that you believe would enhance the health and overall impact of your church's children's ministry volunteer experience?
20. What would you say is your greatest current frustration in serving as a children's ministry volunteer?

Appendix C
IRB Approval

LIBERTY UNIVERSITY
INSTITUTIONAL REVIEW BOARD

October 7, 2013

Kenneth Gene Warren
IRB Exemption 1661.100713: Developing Healthy, High-Impact Children's Ministry Volunteers in the Local Church

Dear Kenneth,

The Liberty University Institutional Review Board has reviewed your application in accordance with the Office for Human Research Protections (OHRP) and Food and Drug Administration (FDA) regulations and finds your study to be exempt from further IRB review. This means you may begin your research with the data safeguarding methods mentioned in your approved application, and that no further IRB oversight is required.

Your study falls under exemption category 46.101 (b)(2), which identifies specific situations in which human participants research is exempt from the policy set forth in 45 CFR 46:

> (2) Research involving the use of educational tests (cognitive, diagnostic, aptitude, achievement), survey procedures, interview procedures or observation of public behavior, unless:
> (i) information obtained is recorded in such a manner that human subjects can be identified, directly or through identifiers linked to the subjects; and (ii) any disclosure of the human subjects' responses outside the research could reasonably place the subjects at risk of criminal or civil liability or be damaging to the subjects' financial standing, employability, or reputation.

Please note that this exemption only applies to your current research application, and that any changes to your protocol must be reported to the Liberty IRB for verification of continued exemption status. You may report these changes by submitting a change in protocol form or a new application to the IRB and referencing the above IRB Exemption number.

If you have any questions about this exemption, or need assistance in determining whether possible changes to your protocol would change your exemption status, please email us at irb@liberty.edu.

Sincerely,

Fernando Garzon, Psy.D.
Professor, IRB Chair
Counseling

(434) 592-4054

LIBERTY
UNIVERSITY.

Liberty University | Training Champions for Christ since 1971

1971 UNIVERSITY BLVD. LYNCHBURG, VA. 24502 IRB@LIBERTY.EDU FAX (434) 522-0506 WWW.LIBERTY.EDU

Appendix D

Volunteer Survey Responses

Table 2

Question[a]	Possible Responses	Results (%)
A healthy volunteer experience is one in which the volunteer displays passion about their service in a way that spiritually impacts others, while also bringing a sense of fulfillment to the volunteer. Are you currently having this type of experience as a volunteer in the children's ministry of your church?	Yes, I am	89.96
	No, I am not	4.35
	Not really sure	0.00
	Other (please specify)	8.70
Can you clearly articulate the vision of your church?[b]	Yes	90.91
	No	4.55
	I can articulate a portion of the vision	4.55
Do you believe the vision statement of the church incorporates the value of children somewhere in its message?	Yes	89.96
	No	4.35
	Not Sure	4.35
	Other	4.35

APPENDIX D: VOLUNTEER SURVEY RESPONSES

Question[a]	Possible Responses	Results (%)
Do you believe your service to the Lord in children's ministry is fulfilling the vision of the church?	Yes	95.65
	No	4.35
	Not Sure	0.00
	Other	0.00
Within your ministry as a children's ministry volunteer do you feel the church emphasizes the task more (changing the dirty diaper) or the ministry more (loving the child) as it relates to your service?	Task More	13.04
	Ministry More	78.26
	Not Sure	8.70
	Other	0.00
Do you believe current volunteer morale is high in the children's ministries of your church? If so, why? If not why?[c]	Open-ended	N/A
Do you believe God has called you to serve in children's ministry?	Yes	89.96
	No	4.35
	Unsure	4.35
	Other	4.35
Do you believe your walk with Christ is growing stronger because of your service to the Lord as a children's ministry volunteer?	Yes	86.96
	No	4.35
	Sometimes	8.70
	Other	0.00
Do you believe your church is invested in developing you as a children's ministry volunteer?	Yes	73.9
	No	8.70
	Sometimes I do	13.04
	Other	8.70

APPENDIX D: VOLUNTEER SURVEY RESPONSES

Question[a]	Possible Responses	Results (%)
Do you know your spiritual gifts and are they being utilized within your children's ministry role?	Yes	91.30
	No	4.35
	I am unsure	4.35
	Other	0.00
If you believed God was leading you to a different area of ministry within the church, do you feel there is freedom to explore this leading from God?	Yes	91.30
	No	8.7
	I am unsure	0.00
	Other	0.00
Do you believe the children's ministry leadership actively shows concern for your personal spiritual development through engagement, strategic planning, and accountability?	Yes	52.17
	No	8.70
	Sometimes	34.78
	Other	8.70
Are victories (wins) celebrated amongst volunteer children's ministry staff? If yes, how so?[b]	Yes	77.27
	No	4.55
	Sometimes	18.18
	Other	40.91d
As a volunteer do you feel supported by your Lead/Sr. Pastor and other pastoral staff members? If yes, how so?	Yes	82.61
	No	4.35
	Sometimes	13.04
	Other	39.13d
Within the last year have you personally been involved in the successful recruiting of another children's ministry volunteer?[b]	Yes	63.64
	No	36.36

109

APPENDIX D: VOLUNTEER SURVEY RESPONSES

Question[a]	Possible Responses	Results (%)
Do you feel the current training for children's ministry in your church is contributing to the development of healthy, high impact children's volunteers?	Yes	39.13
	No	21.74
	Maybe	34.78
	Other	8.70
When serving the Lord in children's ministry do you feel a strong sense that you are being prayed for or are being frequently lifted up in prayer by the church and church staff?[b]	Yes	54.55
	No	13.64
	Sometimes	31.82
	Other	0.00
Which phrase best describes how you feel your ministry is viewed?	I am a ministry volunteer	34.78
	I am a ministry partner	60.87
	I am just fulfilling a role	4.35
	Other	13.04
Name 1 thing that you believe would enhance the health and overall impact of your church's children's ministry volunteer experience?[c]	Open-ended	N/A
What would you say is your greatest current frustration in serving as a children's ministry volunteer?[b]	Open-ended	N/A

[a] All questions received twenty-three responses unless otherwise indicated.

[b] This question received twenty-two responses.

[c] This question received twenty-one responses.

[d] The percentages here do not equal 100 percent because some participants answered one of the first three questions but additionally responded in writing in the "other" category as well.

Appendix E

Pastoral/Ministry Leader Survey Responses

Table 3

Questions[a]	Possible Answers	Results (%)
A healthy volunteer experience is one in which the volunteer displays passion about their service in a way that spiritually impacts others while also bringing a sense of fulfillment to the volunteer. Do you believe your children's ministry volunteers are having a healthy experience serving in the children's ministries of your church?	Our children's ministry volunteers are having a healthy children's ministry volunteer experience.	62.50
	Our children's ministry volunteers are not currently enjoying a healthy volunteer children's ministry experience.	0.0
	I am unsure if our children's ministry volunteers are having a healthy volunteer experience.	0.0
	Other	37.5

APPENDIX E: PASTORAL/MINISTRY LEADER SURVEY RESPONSES

Questions[a]	Possible Answers	Results (%)
Can children's ministry volunteers in your church clearly articulate the vision of the church?	All children's ministry volunteers can articulate the vision.	25.0
	Most children's ministry volunteers can articulate the vision of the church.	62.5
	Some of our children's ministry volunteers can articulate the vision of the church.	12.5
	Our children's ministry volunteers cannot clearly articulate the vision of the church.	0.0
	Other	0.0
Do you believe the vision of the church incorporates the value of children somewhere in its message?	Yes	100.0
	No	0.0
	Other	0.0
Do you believe the children's ministry volunteer's service to the Lord in children's ministry is fulfilling the vision of the church?	Yes	100.0
	No	0.0
	Maybe	0.0
	Other	0.0
Do you feel your church emphasizes the task more or the ministry more as it relates to children's ministry volunteer service?	My church emphasizes the task more. (Volunteers changing diapers)	0.0
	My church emphasizes the ministry more. (Volunteers praying for the children)	62.5
	I am unsure.	0.0
	Other	37.5

APPENDIX E: PASTORAL/MINISTRY LEADER SURVEY RESPONSES

Questions[a]	Possible Answers	Results (%)
Do you believe current volunteer morale is high in the children's ministries of your church? If not why?	Children's ministry volunteer morale is high.	75.0
	Children's ministry volunteer morale is low.	0.0
	I am unsure about the morale of children's ministry volunteers	0.0
	Other	25.0
Does your children's ministry leadership strive to discover if potential volunteers have been called to serve in children's ministry?	Yes	62.5
	No	0.0
	Sometimes	37.5
Do you believe your children's ministry volunteers walk with Christ is growing stronger as a result of their service to the Lord and His church in children's ministry?	Yes	87.5
	No	0.0
	I am not sure	12.5
Does your church invest heavily (finances, prayer, energy, time) into the leadership development of children's ministry volunteers?	Yes	75.0
	No	0.0
	Sometimes	25.0
	Other	12.5
Does your church provide ongoing training/equipping to assist children's ministry volunteers with learning, developing, and then using their spiritual gifts in ministry?	Yes	25.0
	No	12.5
	Sometimes	62.5
	Other	0.0

APPENDIX E: PASTORAL/MINISTRY LEADER SURVEY RESPONSES

Questions[a]	Possible Answers	Results (%)
If God leads a children's ministry volunteer to a different area of ministry within the church, do you feel there is freedom for this volunteer to explore this leading from God?[b]	Always	85.71
	Sometimes	0.0
	Maybe	14.29
	Never	0.0
Does the children's ministry leadership in your church regularly show concern for the personal spiritual development of volunteers through engagement, strategic planning and accountability?	Always	37.5
	Sometimes	62.5
	Never	0.0
	Other	0.0
Are victories (wins) celebrated in the children's ministry of your church? If yes, how so?	Always	62.5
	Sometimes	50.0
	Never	0.0
	Other	25.0
As a Pastor do you believe that you adequately support (prayer, encouragement, presence etc.) the children's ministry and children's ministry volunteers of your church?	Yes	75.0
	No	0.0
	Sometimes	12.5
	Other	12.5
Within the last year has the successful recruiting of children's ministry volunteer been more staff driven or volunteer driven (In other words who do you feel is most responsible for new children's ministry volunteers)?	Staff	75.0
	Volunteer	12.5
	No recruiting efforts have taken place	0.0
	Other	25.0

APPENDIX E: PASTORAL/MINISTRY LEADER SURVEY RESPONSES

Questions[a]	Possible Answers	Results (%)
Do you feel the current training for children's ministry volunteers in your church is contributing to the development of healthy, high impact children's volunteers?	Yes	62.5
	No	0.0
	I am unsure	37.5
How much of a priority is church-wide prayer for the children's ministry and children's ministry volunteers in your church?	Extremely important	0.0
	Important	50.0
	Somewhat important	37.5
	Not that important	12.5
	Other	0.0
Name 1 thing that you believe would enhance the health and overall impact of your church's children's ministry volunteer's experience?	Open-ended	N/A
What would you say is your greatest current frustration with anything related to children's ministry volunteers in your church?	Open-ended	N/A

[a] All questions were answered by eight respondents unless otherwise indicated.
[b] This question received seven responses.

Bibliography

12Stone Church. "Children's Ministry Volunteer Training." 12Stone Church Resources. https://resources.12stone.com/elementary/childrens-ministry-volunteer-training.
———. "Volunteers." 12Stone Church Resources. https://resources.12stone.com/tag/Volunteers.
Adams, Steve. *Children's Ministry on Purpose: A Purpose-Driven Approach to Lead Kids toward Spiritual Health.* Grand Rapids: Zondervan, 2017.
Anderson, Leith, and Jill Fox. *The Volunteer Church: Mobilizing Your Congregation for Growth and Effectiveness.* Grand Rapids: Zondervan, 2015.
Baird, Greg. "7 Things We Need To Understand About Training Volunteers." Children's Ministry Leader. http://childrensministryleader.com/training-volunteers/.
Barna, George. *Transforming Children into Spiritual Champions.* Ventura: Regal, 2003.
Beckwith, Ivy. *Postmodern Children's Ministry: Ministry to Children in the 21st Century.* El Cajon: Youth Specialties, 2004.
Brown, Daniel Alan, and Craig Brian Larson. *The Other Side of Pastoral Ministry: Using Process Leadership to Transform Your Church.* Grand Rapids: Zondervan, 1996.
Cacciofli, Peter, and Pattimari Sheets Cacciofli. *History of the Old Classic Children's Stories.* Raleigh: Lulu, 2012.
Cloud, Henry. *The Power of the Other: The Startling Effect Other People Have on You, From the Boardroom to the Bedroom and Beyond—And What to Do about It.* New York: Harper Business, 2016.
Cousins, Don. *Experiencing Leadershift: Letting Go of Leadership Heresies.* Colorado Springs: Cook, 2008.
Crosby, Robert G., III, and Erin I. Smith. "Church Support as a Predictor of Children's Spirituality and Prosocial Behavior." *Journal of Psychology and Theology* 43.4 (Winter 2015) 243–54. http://journals.biola.edu/jpt/volumes/43/issues/4/articles/243.
Eisner, David, et al. "The New Volunteer Workforce." *Stanford Social Innovation Review.* https://ssir.org/articles/entry/the_new_volunteer_workforce.

Ervin, Andrew. *Best Practices for Children's Ministry*. Kansas City: Beacon Hill, 2010.

Falwell, Jonathan. *InnovateChurch*. Nashville: B&H, 2008.

Finzel, Hans. *The Top Ten Mistakes Leaders Make*. Petaling Java: Advantage Quest, 2008.

Flanagan, Joan. *The Successful Volunteer Organization: Getting Started and Getting Results in Nonprofit, Charitable, Grass Roots, and Community Groups*. Chicago: Contemporary, 1984.

Geiger, Eric. "Leaving A Legacy of Leadership, How Moses Developed Leaders." https://ericgeiger.com/2015/06/leaving-a-legacy-of-leadership-how-moses-developed-leaders/.

Gerson, Richard. *Achieving High Performance: A Research-Based Practical Approach*. Amherst: HRD, 2006.

Hall, Chad W., et al. *Faith Coaching: A Conversational Approach to Helping Others Move Forward in Faith*. Hickory: Coach Approach Ministries, 2009.

Ham, Ken C., et al. *Already Gone: Why Your Kids Will Quit Church and What You Can Do to Stop It*. Green Forest: Master, 2009.

Hancox, Bob, et al. *Coaching for Engagement: Achieving Results through Powerful Conversations*. Vancouver: Tekara Organizational Effectiveness, 2010.

Haywood, Janice A. *Enduring Connections: A Children's Ministry that Weaves*. Saint Louis: Bookmasters, 2007.

Heusser, D. B. *Helping Church Workers Succeed: The Enlistment and Support of Volunteers*. Valley Forge: Judson, 1980.

Houser, Tina. *Building Children's Ministry: A Practical Guide*. Nashville: Thomas Nelson, 2008.

Howard, Lynne. "Keeping Your Children's Ministry Volunteers." http://www.lynnehoward.com/home/keeping-your-childrens-ministry-volunteers.

Hybels, Bill. *The Volunteer Revolution: Unleashing the Power of Everybody*. Grand Rapids: Zondervan, 2004.

Ingersoll, Heather Nicole. "Making Room: A Place for Children's Spirituality in the Christian Church." *International Journal of Children's Spirituality* 19.3/4 (2014) 164–78. doi:10.1080/1364436X.2014.979774.

Kang, Minjeong. "Moderating Effects of Identification on Volunteer Engagement." *Journal of Communication Management* 20.2 (2016) 102–17. doi:10.1108/jcom-08-2014-0051.

Keeley, Robert J. *Helping Our Children Grow in Faith: How the Church Can Nurture the Spiritual Development of Kids*. Grand Rapids: Baker, 2008.

Kennedy, John W. "The 4-14 Window." *ChristianityToday*, July 1, 2004. http://www.christianitytoday.com/ct/2004/july/37.53.html.

Kinnaman, David, and Aly Hawkins. *You Lost Me: Why Young Christians Are Leaving Church—And Rethinking Faith*. Grand Rapids: Baker, 2011.

Knox, John. *John Wesley's 52 Standard Sermons: An Annotated Bibliography*. Eugene: Wipf & Stock, 2017.

Knox, John. *Sacro-Egoism: The Rise of Religious Individualism*. Eugene: Wipf & Stock, 2016.

BIBLIOGRAPHY

Lawrenz, Mel. *Spiritual Influence: The Hidden Power Behind Leadership.* Grand Rapids: Zondervan, 2012.

Mancini, Will. *Church Unique: How Missional Leaders Cast Vision, Capture Culture, and Create Movement.* San Francisco: Jossey-Bass, 2008.

Mavity, Chris. *Your Volunteers: From Come and See to Come and Serve.* N.p.: Self-published, 2014. Kindle ed.

May, Scottie. *Children Matter: Celebrating Their Place in the Church, Family, and Community.* Grand Rapids: Eerdmans, 2005.

Morgan, Tony, and Tim Stevens. *Simply Strategic Volunteers: Empowering People for Ministry.* Loveland: Group Publishing, 2005.

Newell, Al. "Seven Reasons Why Volunteer Ministries Fail." http://www.newellandassociates.com/seven-reasons-why-volunteer-ministries-fail/.

North Point Community Church. "History." http://northpoint.org/about/history.

North Point Ministries. "Children's Environments." https://insidenorthpoint.org/children/.

Power, John. *The Rise and Progress of Sunday Schools: A Biography of Robert Raikes and William Fox.* London: Forgotten Books, 2012.

Rainer, Thom S., and Eric Geiger. *Simple Church: Returning to God's Process for Making Disciples.* Nashville: B&H, 2011.

Richards, Larry. *A Theology of Children's Ministry.* Grand Rapids: Zondervan, 1983.

———. *Children's Ministry: Nurturing Faith within the Family of God.* Grand Rapids: Ministry Resources Library, 1988.

Searcy, Nelson. *Healthy Systems, Healthy Church.* Church Leader Insights, 2010. Kindle ed.

Searcy, Nelson, and Jennifer Dykes Henson. *Connect: How to Double Your Number of Volunteers.* Grand Rapids: Baker, 2012.

Sinek, Simon. *Start with Why: How Great Leaders Inspire Everyone to Take Action.* London: Portfolio, 2013.

Stanley, Andy, et al. *7 Practices of Effective Ministry.* Sisters: Multnomah, 2004.

Stoltzfus, Tony. *Leadership Coaching: The Disciplines, Skills and Heart of a Christian Coach.* Virginia Beach: Self-published, 2005.

Thomas, Scott, and Tom Wood. *Gospel Coach: Shepherding Leaders to Glorify God.* Grand Rapids: Zondervan, 2012.

Watterson, Danny. "Why High Capacity Children's Pastors Are So Hard to Find." https://www.vanderbloemen.com/blog/why-high-capacity-childrens-pastors-are-so-hard-to-find.

Wideman, Jim. *Children's Ministry Volunteers That Stick.* Loveland: Group Publishing, 2004.

Williams, Dennis E., and Kenneth O. Gangel. *Volunteers for Today's Church: How to Recruit and Retain Workers.* Eugene: Wipf & Stock, 2004.

Wuest, Kenneth S. *Wuest's Word Studies from the Greek New Testament: For the English Reader.* Grand Rapids: Eerdmans, 1974.

Index

12Stone Church, viii, 71–72, 77, 82–84, 117
12Stone Church of Lawrenceville, Georgia; 77, 82
7 Practices of Effective Ministry, 23, 66n27, 68n28, 69n29, 80n2, 119

Al Newell, 18–19, 119
Andy Stanley, 23, 80, 119
Awana, 64, 88, 96

Barna Group, 9
Bill Hybels, 63, 118
Bob Nelson, 57

Chad Hall, Bill Cooper and Kathryn McElveen, 24
children's ministry volunteer, 101, 117–19
clarity gap, 64–65
Clergy, 5, 17, 47
coach, xii, 21, 24–25, 49, 51–52, 55–60, 75, 82–83, 86, 91–96, 118–19
Craig Larson, 53, 117
Crossings Community Church of Oklahoma City, Oklahoma; 77–79

D. B. Huesser, 59
Daniel, 3–4
David Kinnaman, 10, 21, 118

Dennis Williams and Kenneth Gangel, 25, 119
Dwight L. Moody, 30

Early Modern Period, 6
Eric Geiger, 61, 118–19

George Barna, 9, 13, 19, 117
Greg Baird, 74, 117

Hancox, Hunter, and Boudreau, 58
Hans Finzel, 65, 118
Heather Ingersoll, 15, 118
holding tank, 13–14
house churches, 8, 14

Industrial Revolution, 6
Institutional Review Board (IRB), 32
Ivy Beckwith, 8, 22, 117

Janice Haywood, 22, 118
Jesus, xii, 1–2, 4–5, 8, 10, 14, 20, 26–27, 30, 58–59, 68, 81
Jethro, 28–29
Jim Wideman, 20, 119
Johnathan Wesley, 7, 118

katartizō, 13
Ken Ham, 12, 118

Lawrence Richards, 20
Lay ministry, 5–7, 15, 46, 88
Lynn Howard, 82, 118

INDEX

Martin Luther, 6
Matt Wilmington, 56
Medieval Era, 5
Middle Ages, 5
ministry partner, 38, 46–48, 56, 103, 105, 110
Minjeong Kang, 23, 118
Modern Period, 6–7
Moses, 3, 27–29, 118

Nelson Searcy, 51, 53, 119
North Point Church of Alpharetta, Georgia; 77, 79

Reformation, 6
Renaissance, 6
Robert Keeley, 118
Robert Raikes, 7–8, 119

Saddleback Church of Lake Forest, California; 77, 85
Scott Thomas, 21, 119
Simon Sinek, 61, 119
Southern Baptist Conservatives of Virginia (SBCV), 32
Steve Adams, 85–86, 117

Sunday school, 2, 7–8, 12, 98, 119
SurveyMonkey, 32–33, 39

the Journey Church in New York City, 79
Thomas Road Baptist Church, 56
Tim Stevens, 20, 119
Tina Houser, 22, 118
Tom Wood, 21, 119
Tony Morgan, 20, 119

UpStreet children's ministry, 80–82

vacation Bible school, 63, 89
Volunteer, iii-iv, viii, x, xii-xiii, 1, 3–9, 11, 13–96, 101–5, 107–115, 117–19
volunteer dysfunction, 14, 18, 44, 58, 60, 96

Will Mancini, 64, 119
William Fox, 7, 119
Wooddale Church in Eden Prairie, Minnesota; 79
Word of Life, 8

www.ingramcontent.com/pod-product-compliance
Lightning Source LLC
Chambersburg PA
CBHW071448160426
43195CB00013B/2054